# The Woman who CENSORED CHURCHILL

*Dedicated to David and Martin*
*and remembering the many thousands*
*of Londoners who perished*
*between 1940 and 1945*

# The Woman who CENSORED CHURCHILL

## RUTH IVE

The History Press

Disclaimer: This work is based on the author's recollection and every effort has been made to remain true to her experiences of the time. The publishers and the author have made every effort to clear permission for all images and documents reproduced within the work. However, we apologise for any erroneous use of copyrighted material and would welcome contact from the original copyright holder.

First published 2008

The History Press Ltd
The Mill, Brimscombe Port
Stroud, Gloucestershire, GL5 2QG
www.thehistorypress.co.uk

British Library Cataloguing in Publication Data.
A catalogue record for this book is available from the British Library.

ISBN 978 0 7524 4716 2

Printed in Great Britain

# CONTENTS

# INTRODUCTION

Around 1988, I thought that as more official documents were being released into the Public Domain, it was time for me to tell and write about the important role played by MI9, known publicly as The Postal and Telegraph Censorship. This included in its various remits the Transatlantic Radio Line which operated between this country, America, Canada and, for a short period, Cairo from 1941–1945. It had been rumoured for some years that this 'hotline radio link' between Churchill and Roosevelt existed but, in spite of the speculation and some highly coloured rumours, no accurate account of its existence has been recorded. I believed that a personal glimpse of our wartime leaders, including their characters and work styles, would be of historic interest and would reveal the everyday realities of listening in to history.

I had just retired from my job with a radio and television news agency and, after twenty-six years, I missed the discipline of a work routine. This, I thought, would be an interesting short-term hobby to fill my retirement days. How wrong I could be! By 2005, the long trail to find the true history of wireless and telegraphic interceptions and the technology that accompanied it was finally revealed, and I could truly declare 'mission accomplished'.

*Ruth Magnus Ive*
*2008*

# PROLOGUE

Although I had spent three and a half years listening to a terrible war being planned, organised and executed, listening in to the voices of Winston Churchill, Franklin Roosevelt and all the major statesmen and characters of that era, unbelievable as it may seem now, when I left my job as Censor on the Transatlantic Link in the Radio Department of the Postal and Telegraph Censorship, I was so quickly immersed into the life of an ordinary suburban housewife that I almost forgot the historical implications of my wartime work. The past became so deeply buried and seemed quite unreal when contrasted with my own rather ordinary domestic life, but nevertheless, when I watched old films and newsreels, read the War memoirs of the famous, I began to realise that I too had a story to tell of those extraordinary war years. So many of us, in our teens and early twenties when the War started, experienced that incredible division in our lives.

Even now it makes me shudder to think of instant decisions I had to make and the responsibilities I had to shoulder. I can only suppose it was the insouciance of youth that got me through.

The vow of silence imposed by the Official Secrets Act doesn't exactly encourage chatter, and I wanted to play the game according to the rules, so only my family and a few friends knew about my wartime work. While reading those biographies and memoirs of the famous, I became aware that if the Transatlantic Radio Service was referred to at all, it was described either inaccurately or imprecisely, and I thought it would be of interest to many people for me to recall an account of the happenings of the Department.

So after various skirmishes with Government Departments in an effort to free myself from the Official Secrets Act, I am now able to reveal the activities of one of the least known secret communication channels of the War.

In fact, I had started to give short talks to private clubs when BBC Radio approached me to do a broadcast. To try to recapture something of that particular wartime atmosphere, I returned to look at the building where I worked in St Martin's Le Grande in the City of London – virtually under the shadow of St Paul's Cathedral, and to my surprise, found the exterior of the building little changed, just forty-five years' more dirt on its stonework, the wartime wire netting on the doors and windows still in place.

I pushed open the door and found a lone civil servant messenger sitting at a desk in the entrance hall who told me when I said I had worked in this building during the War, how lucky I was to come in now for the building was just about to be pulled down. I told Cathy Drysdale, my BBC producer, of Union House's imminent fate and she promptly decided that the talk would have far more bite to it if it was made in situ, so she set about gaining permission from the landlord.

I assumed that the building was still owned by the Post Office who had bequeathed it to British Telecom, but they told Cathy they had just sold to a Japanese bank, while they in turn told her of the sale of Union House to a property company. However, the property company was both sympathetic and interested and immediately gave their permission for the broadcast to be done there.

On one very cold and windy January day, Cathy Drysdale, June Knox Mawer and myself, plus recorder, microphones and assorted pieces of equipment, unlocked the doors of the now completely empty Union House. There was no electricity laid on, so by the light of a torch, we found and pushed open the creaking ground-floor door to the old 'Operations' room and entered.

I could scarcely believe my eyes – the place hadn't changed since I walked out in July 1945. True, somebody had taken down those old trestle tables, removed the desks and emptied those always-full ashtrays, and then – just left the place. Even the Colonel's partitioned office was still there, that old brown Ministry of Works lino was still on the floor, those dreadful early florescent tube lights that always emitted a shrill buzz, all preserved under layers of dust and dirt.

I was completely shattered, and worst of all for a broadcast, rendered practically speechless. It seemed incredible that the building could have survived – it only just survived in the Blitz when a parachute mine dropped on Armour House next door damaging our roof, but it got patched up and our Censorship Departments only occupied the ground floor. It also escaped 'redevelopment' and 'refurbishment' and all the other things they do to buildings these days.

For two hours I recorded my memories. The torchlight was fading, we were very cold and it was time to leave. I told Cathy and June that we should surely tip-toe out of the room so as not to disturb the ghosts, for if ever a building deserves to be haunted by voices, this one did.

# 1

# LIFE IN 1938/9

My parents were dedicated theatre and opera lovers, thinking nothing of donning full evening dress to go by train via Fenchurch Street Station to the theatre and opera in London from Westcliff-on-Sea, where we lived till I was sixteen. They even allowed me to attend the Guildhall School of Music and Drama, though when it came to the crunch my father, in real Barrett of Wimpole style, told me in no uncertain way that no daughter of his was going on the stage.

I was furious at this decision. I had made no secret of this ambition; my parents had taken me to every suitable production at Southend Hippodrome since I was six and up to London for matinees for special occasions, not to mention regular Saturday afternoons spent in the cinema. I had wept buckets at *Bitter Sweet* with Peggy Wood in the lead; had been thrilled at Matheson Lang in a play called *The Bungalow*; and was taken to London to see the Diaghaliev ballets, so I was thoroughly immersed in stagecraft and music by the time I was sixteen.

At the Guildhall, I discovered I wasn't particularly interested in playing either heroines or insipid *ingénue* parts, but what really fascinated me were the comedy and character roles and particularly vocal techniques – inflations, pauses, timing, playing for laughs and tears and how the voice alone can be used as an instrument to stir the imagination.

In the 1930s we did not lack examples of this craft. Voices continually assailed our ears from the cinema newsreels and the wireless, from Hitler's rantings to the intimate storytelling of A.J. Alan. Our ears became our sixth sense, sensitive and attuned to nuances of tone.

I did enjoy my time there. It was a relief to leave my all-girl, very strict school and mix with girls and *boys* with similar tastes, similar ambitions, and quite a few had made considerable financial sacrifices to enjoy their musical and stage education. No grants then. I did my vocal exercises with enthusiasm, learning that the vocal chords had to be treated and cared for as a musical instrument, and I remember my teacher, Horace Sequira, shouting at me from the other end of the auditorium: 'Project! Project! I want to hear every syllable'. Sometimes, sitting at the National Theatre – now with earphones clamped to my head – I wish they could have heard Mr S. at full steam. The only blip came when I was reading a sonnet to my very elderly Shakespeare teacher when he dropped dead: a quite terrifying experience. Endless ribbing about my 'drop dead performance'.

I was in a couple of stage productions. One, a German play called *Matchen in Uniform*, was about lesbian love in a girls' school, playing the part of a schoolgirl infatuated with another. My parents were not impressed.

But my cultural tastes were not formed at the Guildhall; Colonel de Basil's Company of The Ballet Russe de Monte Carlo were on a London visit and I think I saw every production from the gallery seat that I had queued for. Music from Stravinski, Ravel, Poulence, Debussy, backdrops by Derain and Bakst, and dancers such as Massine and Lifar; the entire genre I found stimulating – and still do. It seemed to me then that the 1930s were a turning point in the arts and everything was about to change, and in my own life too.

I was an only child of parents from a very close-knit but ever-quarrelling Jewish family and my father's conception of a dutiful daughter was not – as he put it – 'gallivanting around England ON HER OWN', but staying at home, helping my mother, getting a nice teaching job and marrying the right young Jewish man when the time came. My mother was far more sympathetic and understanding, remembering her own struggle to live an independent life before she was married. She was a born businesswoman and administrator and in her single days before the First World War, had opened and managed one of the first chains of exclusive off-the-peg dress shops for a Bond Street firm. Her sister was even more adventurous in her business life, doing a similar job but opening a chain of lingerie shops in America, so I did have two shoulders to cry on.

Obviously, I made a real drama out of the situation, sulking around the place for months till my father, tiring of this constant stage performance, told me I must go to commercial school to learn shorthand and typing so that 'I would have something at the back of me', and then he might reconsider the situation.

By this time, we had moved back to London and lived in a large rambling flat in Hampstead. Still muttering under my breath that I didn't want to be a shorthand typist, I was enrolled at the Gregg School of Commerce in Finchley Road for the new term starting in September 1938. However, in the August, a tragedy occurred that changed the course of my life.

In the '30s, my mother's cousin, Bernard Davidson, devoted a great deal of his time working at Bloomsbury House trying to help our German and Austrian brethren escape from Nazi tyranny, and as we had a couple of extra bedrooms, we gave hospitality to quite a few of these poor people for a short time before they moved on to more permanent homes. Among them was Erica Kaufmann, a girl my own age who arrived in England alone, leaving her widowed mother and younger sister behind in Aachen where they lived. Erica and I got on very well together, and she hoped her family would soon join her and together they would all go on to America. Then suddenly, without any apparent reason, Mrs Kaufmann's letters to her daughter stopped. Naturally enough, Erica was demented with worry. So my father and cousin Bernard devised a plan that they hoped would give Erica peace of mind and help her mother and sister leave Germany.

As it was August, it was arranged that I should go with my parents on holiday to a Belgian seaside resort – Knoccke, I think it was – where my father would put me on the Ostende train bound for Germany. Erica had returned there a few days earlier (her British visa was still valid), and she would meet me off the train. I was to try to persuade the whole family to leave Germany at the end of my visit, and my father hoped the sight of my British passport would influence the German Customs' officials to allow the Kaufmann family through to freedom.

Privately, I was amazed at my father agreeing to send me on such a journey when he was so insistent that I came home at 10.30pm, even if I just went to a local cinema with a friend – and never mind if the big picture hadn't ended; if a boyfriend was involved, then serious negotiations as to time, venues, etc. had to take place, and even if I was ten minutes late, trouble lay ahead. So, I jumped at this opportunity for adventure and freedom and it never crossed my mind that there were any risks attached – for, of course, I was carrying my British passport, my guarantee of safety.

The first part of the scheme went according to plan and Erica met me off the train at Aachen, looking far more cheerful than she did when we had parted in London. She immediately cleared up the mystery of why her mother had stopped writing to her; apparently she wanted to marry a man who was waiting for his divorce to come through and she didn't know how to break the news to her daughter. 'Was that all?' I said incredulously.

So with that out of the way, I phoned the news through to my parents who were by then back in London, my father telling me to stay in Aachen for a week to see for myself how things were and to try to persuade the Kaufmanns to leave Germany with me.

Perhaps because Aachen was a border town it seemed full of Storm Troopers, Wehrmacht, Hitler Youth, Black- and Brown-shirted troops marching around the place and I was disturbed by the feeling of menace just walking in the main street. The Kaufmanns hadn't dared go to the cinema for months, but they judged it would be safe enough if we went in the back seats of the circle and only spoke English to each other. They particularly wanted to see the film showing at the local cinema, a very long epic that I found extremely boring as I didn't understand German. The newsreel, however, was far from boring; it carried extracts from Hitler's latest speech being rapturously received by a huge audience and an item showing a local Jewish shop being smashed up. It was a relief to get out into the street and I felt that we were all too vulnerable to have gone there in the first place. I was finding my stay in Germany a far more disturbing experience than I had wished.

The telephone ringing at seven o' clock the next morning woke me and I had an overwhelming feeling, a presentiment, that all was not well at home. There comes experiences in life that are so crucial to one's future that they are etched deep into memory and even now I can relive every moment of that hot August day.

I heard whispering voices outside my bedroom door and then Mrs Kaufmann entered, telling me that my cousin, Edward Lobel, had rung from London asking me to take the first train home as my father had been taken seriously ill.

Within the next couple of hours, the Kaufmann family had to make momentous decisions. My father's wish for me to bring Erica, her sister Renata and their mother out of Germany was now obviously impractical. Their dilemma lay as to whether Erica should accompany me back to England but she finally decided her place was with her family, and to take a chance that their American visa (which Mrs Kaufmann's future husband had applied for) would come through before her valid British visa expired.

We said our tearful goodbyes at Aachen station. The platform was crowded with men in all sorts of uniforms and I was thankful to leave. I had seen enough of the Nazi regime and I found it menacing and frightening.

Some hours later, Edward met me at Victoria station and told me my father had died from a massive heart attack the previous evening. A few weeks later the Kaufmann family left Aachen for America.

I was utterly devastated by the entire experience. My father was a forceful personality, a big man with a big voice and sense of humour (and temper) to match, who completely dominated our household. He was at his happiest when listening to music and my earliest memory of him was when I was about two years old, sitting on his lap and shrieking with laughter at 'The Factotum's Song' from *The Barber of Seville* as it played on the gramophone. Our lives would seem dull and quiet without him.

The trip to Germany was a chilling one indeed and brought home with startling clarity the uncertainty and dread of tomorrow that had become part of the daily lives of our German brethren. Nobody could then envisage the appalling horrors of the Holocaust, but nobody could convince me after that visit that Hitler's aims were peaceful. There was an all-pervasive air of aggression and militancy around, which was quite alien to us in England, and I believed the ultimate aim of the Nazi regime was war.

Almost overnight I changed from a rather frivolous, self-centred teenager to a more sensible and realistic young woman. We were not well off now and I knew I would have to get a job, earn a living and make my own way in the world, so when term actually started in September 1938, my attitude had changed radically and I was eager to get started.

Back again then to full-time schooling with classes in bookkeeping, typing and shorthand. Bookkeeping remained a complete mystery to me then (as it does now); typing lessons were amusing, banging away on old Underwood machines to 'The Toreadors Song' played on an equally ancient wind-up gramophone, but shorthand I found quite fascinating. I must have had particularly enthusiastic teachers to get me fired up, for when I left school in July 1939 I had reached a verbatim speed of about 160 to 180 words per minute – the speed of spoken speech. I have since wondered why I found shorthand outlines easy to remember and easy to translate so rapidly onto paper. Again, I suppose it is this facility to react quickly to the spoken word. I was wondering how to put my one and only skill to some use other than a purely commercial one when war broke out in September.

Now I made strenuous efforts to find a job. I laid down terms of reference for my future career, which ideally would provide me with varied and interesting work, adventure, excitement, foreign travel, be socially rewarding and of course, be very well paid, but I soon found out that no prospective employer evinced any interest in me whatsoever until I mentioned my shorthand speeds. Then either the Civil Service Personnel Officer or the commercial company offered the usual routine jobs of shorthand typist/very junior secretary. So I decided to forget the shorthand and look for other ways of earning a living.

Until my ideal offer turned up, I took a temporary secretarial job with an accountant friend of the family, which confirmed my worst fears on the dullness of typing out columns of figures, and I spent the rest of my time helping at the Victoria station canteen – usually washing up – and job hunting. I had by now added another job specification to my list – it must further the war effort.

In the previous spring in 1939, my cousin Edward Lobel, a commercial linguist, had been recruited to join a small nucleus of staff making preliminary arrangements to resuscitate the Postal and Telegraph Censorship that had operated very successfully in the First World War and which had provided excellent Intelligence and information gained from the interception of telegraphic material and the reading of mail.

Edward told me the Censorship was now looking for 'well-educated staff' and thought (rather doubtfully) that I should apply, and brought me home a long application form to fill in.

Very few of the questions on it actually seemed to apply to me: 'had I seen previous war service?' or 'in what other capacity had I served the Empire?' Obviously the Censorship was looking for a far older and more experienced type of personnel, but I did my best and sent my somewhat empty-looking form off and waited but – rather to my surprise – not for very long.

In about the spring of 1940, I was asked to attend an interview at the Censorship Headquarters, which was then housed in the Prudential Building in Holborn in the City of London. Three rather grand gentlemen awaited me: one was a very senior naval officer and I was suitably impressed and distinctly nervous. They asked me the usual routine questions about background, schooling and interests, then the naval gentleman looked at the 'special skills' section on the application form that I had left empty and said somewhat irritably: 'surely you can do something?' Well … no. I was – and still am for that matter – a wretched linguist, so in desperation, I admitted to my shorthand speeds, now getting a bit rusty through lack of practice.

Unaccountably to me, my interviewers showed considerable interest and also in the fact that I wrote Gregg shorthand which is the system mostly used in America. One at a time they fired off a series of Trivial Pursuit-type questions as a general knowledge test and then sent me off to the waiting room while they deliberated. When recalled, my interviewers told me that I would be employed as an Examiner Grade II, and though I was not going to work as a shorthand typist, they suggested that while my application was being processed, I should keep my shorthand speed up by doing temporary secretarial work. I seem to remember that the personnel officer fixed me up with a secretarial job at a Board of Trade department in Furnival Street, opposite.

It seemed to me that this was a very odd sort of job I was going to do but I found the three gentlemen far too awe-inspiring to dare ask any questions.

I spent some months at the Import Licensing Department doing undemanding work with pleasant people but I was very much aware that the Censorship was functioning and investigating my blameless past. Both referees given on my application form phoned my mother to say they had been visited and questioned by members of the Special Branch and wondered what on earth I was going to do. I had to admit that I had only got a job at the Censorship but as I had already signed – like every other person in the country – The Official Secrets Acts, I didn't go into details. Privately, I was equally mystified.

Looking back and with hindsight, I realised that I had been sent to a 'safe house' while my blameless past was investigated. I did very little work because my boss only came in about twice a week to check some licensing and rarely dictated a letter. I was grateful for inactivity because the drama of Dunkirk was unfolding hourly. I brought in a wireless to work so we could all keep abreast of the news. My then boyfriend (later my fiancé and eventually, six years later, my husband) was at an army training course in Folkestone and went missing. He reappeared three days later having been sent to the French beaches on the holding operation, returning in one piece though suffering from sea-sickness (he was a dreadful sailor). Thankfully however the Channel was like a mill pond and so the rescue of so many of our troops was a miracle. Winston Churchill, our recently-elected Prime Minister, stirred our emotions and resolve and turned around a stunned country into a united nation, and that is the way it stayed for the next six long years.

# 2

# THE POSTAL CENSORSHIP

I received my call to the Postal and Telegraph Censorship, then housed in its large distinctive red-brick building next door to Gamages in Holborn Circus, in 1941. The worst of the Blitz was over, but it was still something of an obstacle race getting to work every day. Holes would appear in roads that were intact the previous night, trains would suddenly stop and eventually crawl into the next station usually making all the passengers disembark; in fact, public transport was so erratic that often the quickest way to arrive at work was to walk. I was always amazed how quickly glass-strewn streets would get swept up and roads often impassable in the morning were quite cleared when it was time to return home.

All of us new entrants had to undergo a week's training. We were ushered into our school, seated at long trestle tables (later I came to realise that trestle tables were the essential furniture requirement for the Censorship, we must have used the entire

Ministry of Work's store), then addressed by an assortment of officials ranging from the high-ranking naval gentleman who introduced me to a nice girl who showed us how to open an envelope without damaging its contents.

According to our lecturer, the Postal and Telegraph Censorship had been formed in the First World War and had earned itself a useful reputation as an adjunct of the Intelligence Services. It seems that under the Geneva Convention of 1926 on the Protocols of War, the protagonists were at liberty to intercept mail en route from either enemy or neutral countries. It was permissible to read the contents of the seized mail, but it had to be resealed and then forwarded to the addressee.

Our naval blockade of the Atlantic and North Sea were well suited to this operation as the bulk of private and commercial mail was carried on merchant shipping belonging to the many maritime nations (there was only a very restricted airmail service in operation), and when our Navy boarded ships for search, the mail bags would be taken and eventually arrive at our building. Outgoing mail from this country was also censored, so this enormous international traffic in mail bags came to rest on the floor of our building, which by mid-1941 was at Princess House in Holborn.

I was quite surprised at most of my fellow entrants; they were so much older than me – except for one girl of my own age who sat next to me. Joyce Armstrong and I became great friends and have remained so to this day. Some of my fellow students had served in the Censorship during the First World War, one even showed me a photograph of what purported to be a huge empty shed lined with trestle tables and mail bags scattered around the floor. I found these ladies and gentlemen (and they were just that) rather patronising and they had little time for young and new recruits; also they were linguists, speaking at least one language fluently and clearly thought the Old Firm was slipping when it engaged such inexperienced youngsters as myself.

I would like now to dispel a famous British myth concerning the Censorship Department. Nobody – but nobody – was ever issued, ever used, ever scratched out with a BLUE PENCIL. Officers in the Armed Forces perhaps used it when censoring their own troops' mail in the field, but our method of dealing with indiscretions was quite different. Each examiner – and my official title was Examiner, Grade III – was issued with a paper knife, one small pair of scissors and a stock of our own personal numbered sticky labels to be used to seal the opened letters after we had read them.

If we found the writer from this country had broken one of the security rules, such as referring in too much detail to enemy bombing of a certain location, or to large-scale troop movements, or even comments on low public morale, after confirmation from our DAC (Deputy Assistant Censor) we were then given permission to incise the offending passage. Too much detail of military operations from incoming troops' mail would receive equally harsh treatment, but on the other hand, if a letter contained information or reference and comment on the War effort of particular interest but of no security risk, then it would be judged worthy of a Submission Form, the pertinent parts of the letter would be copied onto it, the envelope would be resealed with the Examiner's label, and it would proceed on its journey to the addressee.

In fact, the Censorship was a vast information-gathering organisation, collecting Intelligence from around the world. Being a department of the Ministry of Information, there was a large Trade and Commercial Section that gained great insight into the import of war materials to the enemy via the neutral countries and as well as the laundering of payments to and from Germany for these goods. All the departments worked closely with the Ministry of Economic Warfare and Trading with the Enemy Section of the Board of Trade, and information from the Censorship sources was highly valued by them.

At Training School I remember I was instructed on how to detect 'secret writing' in a letter – real Sherlock Holmes stuff – but when shown an example, it was a joke. A large blank discoloured lump in the middle of a piece of notepaper covered in spidery writing that could be seen at first glance by the most short-sighted reader.

However, looking for micro-dot film was quite a different matter. It seems that this method of smuggling information in and out of this country had recently been found in the fold of an envelope of mail written to an address in Portugal, and as these micro-dots were virtually the size of a pinhead, correspondence from and to neutral countries had to be very carefully examined. My friend discovered the first micro-dot concealed in the envelope flap, and I was congratulated for her.

Then issued with a box file containing the tools of our trade, stuffed full of stories of spies and how to detect them, we were posted to our respective departments – Joyce and I sent to 'Troops' Mail', the lowest form of Censorship life.

We took our place at the usual long table seating twelve Examiners with our DAC sitting at the top, just one of, say, twenty housed in a large open-plan floor space. Letters were packed in bundles of twelve awaiting our attention, and when we had finished and dealt with that packet, presumably off they would go to the GPO Sorting Office. There was never any lack of our raw material; the whole world seemed to be writing to each other.

The first thing I had to learn when reading troops' mail was the Language of Love. This consisted of initials of the first letters of words that made up a loving phrase. S.W.A.L.K. and I.T.A.L.Y. translated meant 'Sealed With A Loving Kiss' and 'I Trust and Love You'. There were about a dozen such phrases getting ever more explicit and Alan Bennett used one in a sketch in *Beyond the Fringe* to great effect. N.O.R.W.I.C.H. stood for '[K]nickers Off Ready When I Come Home'.

Troops' mail came from wherever we had troops stationed: Malta, Gibraltar, India, Singapore, RAF personnel training in Canada and America, merchant seamen, and naval mail from all round the world – bag upon bag of it, sorted into little packets continually thudding onto the floor of Princes House. Whether officers or men, all missed their families, but equally they were all convinced of the need to fight and took the attitude of 'let's get it over as quickly as possible'. I came to the conclusion that English men are not natural letter writers. Few, I am sure, had the opportunity of taking pen to paper before, and few seemed to have a natural talent for writing interesting descriptive letters, but I suppose the need for caution and knowing their words would be read by a third person dampened their ardour; anyway they all showed a collective Stiff Upper Lip with the net result that I found the work repetitive and predictable.

However, there was a certain amount of private mail to be read, mostly from Eire, the neutral European countries and America. The Americans especially wrote good newsy letters and I gained my first insight into the American way of life. It was the first time I had ever heard of children's summer camps, while all my correspondents seemed to be either just returning or setting off on another exciting trip involving thousands of miles of driving down highways. How I envied their mobility. When a really well-written, witty and amusing letter arrived at our table – as one did from Noel Coward – it passed from hand to hand till the whole Department had read it. Very belated apologies to the addressee of Mr C's missive for its slight delay en route.

I began to realise that my knowledge of shorthand had been officially remembered for within a very short time letters from all over the world, trade documents, Bills of Freight and Lading, mail of every description started to be delivered to my table, all of them having a few squiggles or hieroglyphics on them that could be, but usually were not, jottings in Gregg shorthand. I spent hours trying to decipher their meaning; mostly they were variations on the Language of Love, sometimes the Navy, the Army and the Air Force got a bit naughty and hoped to escape the Censor's eagle eye revealing information that they shouldn't, but they were the easy ones. It is one thing to read back your own outlines, quite another to accurately translate somebody else's, though I had brought along several shorthand manuals for reference.

One man living in Portugal wrote his entire letter in shorthand; he was a regular correspondent describing his business and social life at length, and as the letter was posted in Portugal where all mail was required to be carefully examined, a complete and accurate translation was required. I thought it was innocuous enough but the Authorities were suspicious and a special watch was put on the correspondence. I was informed (somewhat grandly) that I had become the official Gregg Shorthand reader for the Censorship and given 2/- a week extra.

The fun came in working with such very pleasant people and once the older Examiners had accepted me they couldn't have been more helpful, but they were so formal. I wouldn't have dreamed of addressing them by their first name – Miss Berry, Mrs Maudslay, Miss Hume-Spry. I sat next to a quiet, charming lady who told me about her fabulously talented piano-playing daughter of my own age, and how one day, she knew she would be famous. Her name was Mrs Johnson and she was quite right – her daughter was Moura Lympany.

Despite enjoying myself and making new friends, I had begun to get restive thinking how I could not spend the rest of the War sitting down reading other people's letters; I wanted some excitement, some action. I had become 'Reserved', that is, I was not allowed to change my job for the duration of the War and there was no way in which I could just hand in my notice. Deliverance came in an unexpected way.

I picked up a bundle of letters with a Maltese stamp on them and opened the first, which was from a seaman on a merchant ship anchored off Valetta. It said roughly: 'Dear Mum, I hope you get this letter because I am smuggling it off the ship because we are in quarantine for small pox and two crew have just died.'

I gave a squeak of horror, dropped the letter and rushed to Barbara Berry telling her what had happened. Within half an hour, the messenger who had handled the letter and me were hustled into a taxi taking us to a doctor off Tottenham Court Road who vaccinated us.

I had been vaccinated before and nothing much happened but this time it took with a vengeance. The doctor told me if I needed further medical attention, I was to ring a certain number and not call my own GP. My mother, getting alarmed at my soaring temperature and swollen arm, did just that. Along came a medical officer of health and an infectious diseases specialist who immediately wanted to put me and my mother into quarantine and, to add to the drama, I started coming out in spots. There was a heat wave going on outside and I thought they were just heat spots but the doctors, peering at my chest, were not so sure and wanted to move us both to an isolation hospital outside London. My mother, who could be a very forceful lady indeed when the occasion demanded, pleaded for a few days' grace and sure enough my spots faded, my temperature returned to normal and my arm to its original size.

Returning to work, I was informed by our Chief Personnel Officer, Miss Fletcher, a very tall and elegant lady who reminded me in her manner of my old headmistress, that I had been promoted to a small administrative job in ULD. I was shocked – for somebody who could hardly mutter a few words in French, I seemed a surprising choice.

ULD stood for Uncommon Languages Department. It was the proud boast of its staff that they could read and understand every known language and dialect in the world, and I remember about twenty people sitting at the usual trestle tables reading letters in all sorts of strange writing: Arabic, Mandarin, Chinese, Gujarati, Hindi, Hebrew, Swahili, Yiddish, languages written in the Cyrillic alphabet, all the Slavonic languages – nothing linguistic ever defeated our team. Mostly they were either retired or serving lecturers or professors from the School of Oriental and African Languages and the School of Slavonic Studies. One gentleman, I was told, knew a record number of obscure dialects in Swahili; another had similar skills in Chinese. The room was very, very quiet and the atmosphere resembled that of a reading room at a university library.

Off from this room was my minute office, lined from floor to ceiling with filing cabinets with just enough room for me to reach my desk. I noted with mixed feelings that my shorthand manuals and letters from my Portuguese correspondent had preceded me.

This was where the Censorship Black List was housed; organisations, companies and individuals from all over the world who in some way or another had offended the Wartime Authorities, or who in any way had behaved suspiciously. This included economic wrongdoings and those who were considered to be a threat to our national security; all were listed here on a very detailed card index.

I had become just a super filing clerk keeping the indexes up to date and answering queries sent in from all the Censorship Departments. This was not what I meant by 'action' and after three weeks I longed for troops' mail.

Joyce too had got herself into a similar dead-end job and together we pleaded with the alarming Miss Fletcher to find us a more demanding role; she certainly did – together we left the Postal Censorship and were transferred to the newly-formed Telephone Censorship Unit.

# 3

# INTERNAL CENSORSHIP UNITS

As early as October 1939, the Post Office and the Postal and Telegraph Censorship had discussed plans for an inland telephone censorship, together with the considerable range of systems of monitoring private and commercial calls that would be needed to implement a full-scale security operation for the civilian population of the United Kingdom.

Even before the Occupation of Europe, elaborate emergency schemes, alternative arrangements and various standby schemes were drawn up should either Faraday Building or Union House become non-operational through enemy action. All sorts of contingency plans were made to safeguard the service, including the complete evacuation of the London Censorship Department to the provincial exchanges.

Internal telephone censorship had always been a sensitive issue, even though in wartime our activities were amply covered by the Emergency Powers Act. There was never any public acknowledgement of our existence, let alone that the departments were so highly organised. Public awareness, if anything, was an implicit acceptance and merely a cartoon subject in The Walls Have Ears campaign.

The headquarters of the Inland Telephone Censorship Unit was housed at Union House, St Martin's Le Grande, within the confines of the City of London, and quite the largest section was the Irish Department. One hundred per cent censorship was required on all telephone traffic to and from Northern Ireland and Eire and, from May 1942, to and from the Isle of Wight. The Anglo-Irish Unit in particular was an enormously difficult service to handle and control.

Originally, the traffic and censors were located in the Trunk Exchange, but the routine adopted there was found to be extremely wasteful of trunk time lines, especially as so many of the London/Belfast circuits were appropriated by the Ministry of Defence. So the Unit was moved to Union House where the operational procedure was altered. It was decided that one censor should listen to calls coming through on one circuit continuously. The calls were lined up by the Faraday operator after being pre-booked by the subscriber, and the operator would then inform the censor of telephone numbers being called.

In practice, this was the most complicated of all the systems to administer efficiently. Censors sat on two sides of long tables on which terminals, earphones and a small switch panel were housed – known as a 'listening position'. I suppose there must have been 100 staff working in the entire Unit because of the intricate shift-working system, which recognised that peak traffic hours demanded more staff coverage than weekends, evenings and even at lunchtime, when it was thought that fewer censors were needed. Circuits were opened then closed by the operators whenever traffic demanded.

The Unit was a constant headache to run. Calls came through continuously, and if the censor went missing – even to go to the washroom – that circuit had to be covered for her. A head-cold epidemic played havoc with staffing arrangements. Our supervisors were constantly on the phone to the Faraday operator checking which circuits were open, which were about to close, which had developed faults, how many staff there were to cover the terminals and generally seeing that all the circuits were working properly.

The lines were open twenty-four hours a day, which meant constant adjustments in staffing positions, and it was not an uncommon sight to see the staff of the Irish Section rushing round the room as in some nightmare game of musical chairs looking for their open circuits. Censors were unable to speak to callers, for there was no 'interrupt' facility. There was, however, a small switch on the listening panel that could trigger off a shrill whistle. That too had its problems, before a suitable sound was found that neither deafened the caller or censor nor failed to obliterate speech completely. Callers were only buzzed if they offended against the usual security regulations. Occasionally I helped out in a supervisory capacity on the night shift if they had a staff crisis, and I wondered how the regulars kept sane amid the chaos. Life was only dull on the Irish Section when the censors actually listened to the calls.

In May 1942, all circuits from the mainland to the Isle of Wight were routed through the Censorship but were partially withdrawn in May 1943, though a monitoring service was maintained till March 1945. The Anglo-Irish Censorship ceased its work on 7 June 1945.

Static Telephone Censorship Units were set up in a number of centres around the country. Some operated for a short period just to cover a particularly sensitive event, such as an RAF operation or naval activity; others remained permanently based on the South Coast and port areas, and were housed in the local telephone exchange. Prior to the Invasion, and during that period, units were also opened to cover a 10-mile-wide belt around the coast from Dundee to Milford Haven.

The standard equipment used was usually a small wooden box that housed ten jacks and keys that were then connected to selected trunk and junction circuits. We listened to conversations on a headset and operated the switch panel ourselves, selecting our own circuits indiscriminately when a small flashing light indicated they were in use. However, we had no facility for either toning down or disconnecting conversation when speakers said things they shouldn't – like noting the arrival or departure of ships, or commenting on the size of military convoys seen on roads. It really was censorship conducted on a sampling basis and wasn't an altogether satisfactory method of controlling security.

In the normal course of events, the staff in the Exchange had no idea of our existence as our small office was never located in the main switch-room. We were usually allocated a pokey little room (probably thought to be the broom cupboard) and instructed never to reveal our presence to the permanent staff. It was to such a unit in Southampton that Joyce and I found ourselves based in 1941.

This hush-hush attitude seemed a bit pointless to us when we started monitoring calls. What possible use could it be to anyone, unaware of our hidden existence, listening in to the local population going about its daily business? We could only report security transgressions and write short reports but no action could be taken because calls, especially incoming ones when routed through an exchange other than Southampton, were well nigh impossible to trace. Feedback informed us of the usefulness of the Irish telephone censorship and our Intelligence gained from that source was appreciated. Yet as Static Units were unable to deter anyone they did not seem to us to serve any purpose, except to gauge the level of secure-mindedness of the local population from our written reports of overheard conversations.

If a continual watch was needed for one particular line only, then a warrant had to be obtained from the director of the Postal and Telegraph Censorship authorising it. The watch was usually mounted in the telephone exchange handling traffic in the district.

Of much more practical use were the Mobile Snapcheck Units. These groups consisted of three or four censors who were called out by the Armed Services at very short notice to cover telephone security for a particularly secret military operation, troop movement or an RAF raid. It was thought to be undesirable for civilians to be seen within the main building of army camps and aerodromes, so we were usually put in a small room or more often a Nissen hut adjoining HQ, which had been wired up with a listening panel and where we sidled in and out as unobtrusively as possible.

These operations were usually for a few days' duration, twenty-four hours before whatever was supposed to happen did, and then twenty-four hours afterwards. The circuits most often selected for monitoring were the Officers' Mess, the Sergeants' Mess and NAAFI. In a very high-security operation, a total blackout of the entire switchboard was imposed and our job was to see that this operational silence was maintained.

After a few weeks of listening to the local Southampton populace talking to their friends and relations, we were posted back to London to a small office somewhere near Fetter Lane. This was the base for the Snapcheck Units run by a quite charming Colonel Ffrench, and this was to be home for us while we travelled around the south of the country visiting military camps, RAF stations and naval dockyards.

England seemed to be full up during the war. The trains were always packed tight, one never expected a seat, but it didn't matter; we enjoyed the spirit of comradeship amongst the rucksacks, the sleeping soldiers in the corridors. Everybody, it seemed to us, was looking for somewhere to spend the night. When you have no official identity, cannot put a label on your work, have no official status and a very, very small living allowance, your choice of accommodation is limited to say the least, and Joyce and I ended up in some very curious situations.

After tramping for hours round Marlow in the pouring rain looking for a room, we found ourselves outside the Police Station. Inspiration! To the Station Sergeant we described pathetically our homeless situation and asked if we could spend the night in his nice dry police cell. He was appalled at such a thought.

'Then,' we said, 'we will go into the street outside, start accosting men and creating a public disturbance and you will have to arrest us and put us in a cell for the night.' The Sergeant told us not to be silly and chased us out of the station. I don't remember sleeping on a park bench so I suppose we found a bed somewhere.

Once, told to report to the Oxford Telephone Exchange (I was alone this time), the manager apologised for not being able to find me anything better than a bed in somebody's garden hut. Oxford was overflowing with students and all the Armed Forces seemed to be stationed nearby, but I was somewhat surprised to see that it really was a bed in a shed. The woman who showed it to me watched me suspiciously.

'What do you do?'
'I am on Government war work.'
'What work?'
'I work in a Government Office.'
'Which Office?'
'One in the centre of Oxford.'
'Which Street?' etc.

She didn't believe a word I said.

I spent a cold uncomfortable night and at about 6am decided to find the bathroom in the house. I couldn't believe it – she had locked me in. I yelled and yelled and bashed at the door. Eventually the woman came, shrieking that I was a German spy and she was going to call the Police. I yelled even louder at the stupid woman and after about an hour of this pantomime, she unlocked the door and I fled.

Colonel Ffrench decided this wasn't good enough for 'his girls' and campaigned vigorously on our behalf, with the result that we were accorded Officer status. Along with this came an increased accommodation allowance that was sufficient to pay for a stay in a hotel; a taxi allowance to use to and from our Nissen hut and hotel, a real luxury; as well as a pay increase from £3 10s a week to £4. We were now respectable.

Odd things happened at work too. Sent to RAF North Weald to cover a particularly important low-flying raid on the French coast, I found that the Sergeant had mistakenly wired up the circuits being used by the Norwegian squadron, all chattering away in their mother tongue. The Lance Corporal turned pale when I suggested he change them for the usual NAAFI and Mess ones. 'Not,' he said, 'without the Adjutant's permission.' It took us three days to track down that Adjutant, (he had probably gone on a course), and not one word of English had been heard on our headsets in that time. I had by now acquired the dubious talent of being able to bug a small manual exchange circuit, but that Lance Corporal wouldn't let me near the switch-room. By the time the Adjutant arrived, the raid was over.

Joyce and I spent the summer drifting round south-east England and the South Coast ports doing undemanding work, staying in comfortable hotels and socialising in the bar when off duty. It was too good a time to last – and of course, it didn't. Colonel Ffrench summoned me back to base, where he told me that the formidable Miss Fletcher wanted to see me immediately.

Miss Fletcher smiled at me frostily. 'How is your shorthand speed?' she enquired.

'Well I haven't actually written it for some time now, it's very rusty.'

'Take two weeks off and get your shorthand speed back to verbatim level, make word perfect transcriptions, then report back here.'

I started off again – 'But I don't want to be a …'

But it was no good arguing with Miss Fletcher or even asking her what I was going to do. In wartime, we didn't question orders; we just did what we were told.

I went home, switched on the wireless and during the next fortnight took down in shorthand every news bulletin, war report, *The Brains Trust*; I even had a go with *ITMA* and then transcribed them.

I reported back to Miss Fletcher. A secretary tested me, reading *The Times* leader. I got it down and managed to transcribe it. I was back to about 160 words per minute.

'Report to Lt. Col. Lyon Clark at Union House next Monday,' ordered Miss Fletcher. I had heard vaguely from Colonel Ffrench about the Irish Section at Union House and wondered why I needed shorthand for that work. Very puzzling.

Joyce meanwhile had been sent to a Static Unit at Bristol, which did not please her one bit. Eventually the Censorship acceded to her wish to join the WRNS and she spent the rest of the War enjoying life in Colombo and Aden. The next time we met was at my wedding in 1946.

# 4

# 'THE RADIO DEPARTMENT': HOW IT WORKED

Incredible as it may seem now to an age that takes for granted instant communication and connection to any part of the world by a variety of highly sophisticated telecommunication techniques, during the War no international conventional telephone network existed. Nobody could pick up a telephone receiver and dial the operator to make a connection, let alone punch a few numbers and instantly hear your chosen caller's voice at the other end of the line, for the simple reason that the Post Office had no means of handling such calls. The Atlantic under-sea cable had been severed by the Allies after the fall of France. On the whole, this was no hardship for the general public who were not used to making phone calls to foreign parts – it was just another facility that went missing. For the Government though, such a restriction severely hampered their efforts to run an efficient administration to conduct a global war.

When America entered the War in 1941, the War Cabinet realised it was imperative to have some sort of telephone system operating across the Atlantic. Before that date, in a somewhat informal way, a radio link-up with Washington and Ottawa was in existence, so the GPO was requested to set about improving and increasing the scope of this service in co-operation with the American Telephone and Telegraph Company and The Bell Telephone and Telegraph Company of America and Canada.

At the end of December 1941, Brendan Bracken, the minister for the Ministry of Information and responsible for the Postal and Telegraph Censorship Department, sought the advice of the Wireless Telegraphy Board of the Post Office on the best method of expanding the radio link. As he correctly forecasted, there would now be a considerable increase in the demand for calls between our Government Ministers and Service Chiefs and their opposite numbers in Washington and Ottawa.

Prior to the outbreak of the War, both the GPO and the Bell Telephone Company had been researching and experimenting with voice privacy systems that would protect the speakers against eavesdroppers, but by 1941, the A3 Scrambler used and operated by the American Telegraph and Telephone Company was the only practical method of disguising speech and was used for transatlantic calls.

The Wireless Telegraphy Board responded to Brendan Bracken's request in no uncertain manner. They discussed the matter thoroughly with Post Office engineers, who informed the Board that it was impossible to devise a radio telephone link that gave any real protection to conversations that took place over it. While the A3 Scrambler system made speech perfectly intelligible to the speakers (a considerable achievement in itself), and could withstand casual eavesdropping, a determined electronic engineer with ample resources could easily unscramble the conversations. So, they warned, as far as the enemy was concerned, all radio telephony calls should be looked on as having no more secrecy than if the speakers were using a public phone box. To compound this wretched news, the Board advised Mr Bracken that they were tolerably certain that all calls were monitored by the enemy, who were particularly interested in information contained in our wireless traffic. No device existed, the Board emphasised, that would give real protection to the speakers. In the light of this severe risk to national security, they requested that their report should be brought to the notice of the War Cabinet so that suitable instructions could be drawn up to ensure that nothing of any value to the enemy was ever transmitted over the radio telephone.

This negative pronouncement must have placed Brendan Bracken and the Chief Censor, Sir Edwin Herbert of the Postal and Telegraph Censorship, in a considerable dilemma. They were under pressure from the War Cabinet to deliver an operational transatlantic link-up within weeks, yet the only system the Post Office could provide contained such dire threats to national security that its very installation made it a very questionable asset.

It became obvious that somehow a rigorous system of safeguards and security routines would have to be imposed on a very restricted but very influential panel of speakers. The original list of users allowed access to the service consisted of the Prime Minister, members of the War Cabinet, the Chiefs of the Imperial General Staff, ministers and their Civil Service departmental private secretaries, our royal family and royal families in exile along with their military and civilian leaders.

Sir Edwin's task was not made any easier by the strongly voiced views of the Chiefs of the Imperial General Staff and the heads of security departments, who at their best were somewhat dubious about the entire project. The majority were frankly horrified at the thought of the War Cabinet, with their precise knowledge of military information, casually lifting up the phone receiver to talk to their colleagues in Washington and Ottawa on an open line.

240

## DRAFT MINUTE FROM THE PRIME MINISTER.

I wish to remind my colleagues of the dangers
of using the radio telephone unless due precautions
are taken.   One must assume that every conversation
on the radio telephone is overheard by the enemy.

A recent test check of radio telephone conversations
brings out two points.

First:   that while considerable discretion is
normally used, it is at times when great political
or military events are on foot (and when discretion is
most necessary) that the tendency to take risks is most
manifest.

Secondly:   that users of the radio telephone seem
to believe that the use of rather vague allusions, nick-
names or initials will render indiscretion innocuous.
These allusions offer a very thin disguise, which would
certainly be pierced by the Enemy Intelligence Service,
and the only result of their use/well be to give the
speaker a false sense of security.

The one secure way of conducting a radio telephone
conversation on a secret matter is first to telegraph
in cypher a memorandum in short numbered paragraphs,
and then to conduct the conversation by reference to
those paragraphs.   In order that this practice may not
endanger the security of our cyphers, such telegrams
should always be endorsed by the originator "Re-cypher
in one time-table".

Draft minute from Winston Churchill expressing his concern over security
on telephone calls. (Courtesy of The National Archives, UK.)

On 31 December 1941, Brendan Bracken wrote to the Prime Minister asking him to approve the procedure as outlined by the Chief Telephone Censor and to be used by him, the War Cabinet and the Chiefs of the Imperial General Staff when speaking on the Transatlantic Radio Service. Mr Churchill wrote personally to Brendan Bracken saying he would willingly submit to the proposed rules.

All this time similar arrangements were being drawn up with the American Censorship Department and The American Telephone and Telegraph Company, together with the Canadian Censorship authorities and The Bell Telephone Company of Canada.

Brendan Bracken informed the Prime Minister that similar censorship procedures had been arranged with President Roosevelt, the Vice President and members of his Administration including Harry Hopkins, the President's special envoy, as well as the American ambassador in London and his staff. Members of our embassy in Washington were included, as were members of our Purchasing Mission and other official personnel.

Sir Edwin Herbert was charged to set up the Radio Department, as it was to be known, at Union House, St Martin's Le Grande, where the censors would operate while the telegraphy side of the operation would be handled at Faraday Building.

With the various security departments voicing their apprehension, the Transatlantic Radio Service became official in January 1942. With equal misgivings, I reported for duty and was ushered into the Colonel's office. 'Office' was too grand a description for the two thin wooden walls and half glass door that were erected against the main wall on the ground-floor space occupied by the Radio Department. The Ministry of Works had patched up our partially destroyed building and only the ground floor was habitable – we and the Irish Unit were the sole occupants. From here, the Colonel could survey his empire though his responsibilities were to the Radio Department only.

In the main workplace, there was no daylight. Windows were sandbagged from top to bottom, there was no air-conditioning to clear the semi-permanent fog of cigarette smoke and we were lit by a collection of those old florescent lights that perpetually buzzed when in need of a replacement tube. Furniture was sparse and rudimentary. Two old trestle tables placed end to end with four unpadded wooden chairs were placed against one wall; another two tables and chairs stood a few feet away. On this stood two old black 'Daffodil' type telephones, two pairs of old heavy-duty telephonist's headphones and two small telephone switch panels. There were two other small desks placed end to end against another wall and the usual black one-piece phone.

I had been transferred from a department that was fully furnished with papers – as offices the world over usually are. At the Postal Censorship there were piles of letters in mail bags needing attention, opened letters being read by staff, letters due for postal deliveries, submission forms, rule books, instruction manuals – in fact, ordinary and normal office paraphernalia. Here at Union House, the emptiness, the lack of office detritus was immediately apparent. Very little paperwork on the desks, no notices on the wall, only piles of scrap paper on the trestle tables. That Monday morning humans were scarce too. One man sat at a desk writing out what to me looked like price tickets; another wearing headphones was writing away as if his very life depended on it, while another (without headphones) was copying notes from one pile of scrap paper on to another.

The Colonel hardly resided in luxury either. A desk, a slightly more comfortable chair behind it, a very large filing cabinet, a small table and chair stuck in one corner, in the other, an asbestos-lined shelf on which stood an ancient gas ring with a tin kettle on it and underneath an army camp bed was stowed away. Not much paperwork done here either by the look of it.

Lieutenant Colonel Lyon Clark, Indian Army (Rtd) Assistant Censor and Head of the Radio Department, greeted me frostily. He was of unremarkable physical appearance with a lean wiry physique, a thin face and pointed chin and dark glittering eyes transfixing his listener, which I found distinctly intimidating. He spoke brusquely in a clipped military style in penetrating tones and was obviously a character 'used to dealing with men'. I, on the other hand, was still going through my Barbara Stanwyck phase and had probably overdone the make-up in order to create a good impression. There was no obvious meeting of minds.

The Colonel then proceeded to explain the work of the Department, always emphasising its strict security profile. The actual office routine was quite extraordinary. As little as possible was to be committed to writing, and I never once remember being given an internal memo to read except perhaps one about annual leave; the rules of the office, like everything else referring to our work, was to be memorised from verbal instructions. There was no book of house rules. I would be receiving only spoken security briefings and I must never put queries referring to the work onto paper and must only discuss the problems that might arise from time to time with Bill Fiske, who was to be my Duty Officer and would explain rota duties and methods of work. I was left in no doubt of my own fate if I broke the rules. I must never mention the true nature of my work, never talk about the contents of the conversations I should be listening to and never reveal the whereabouts of the office. I should tell my mother as few details as I could, sufficient only to satisfy her natural curiosity.

'I have decided,' said the Colonel, 'that as you have been recommended for your fast and accurate shorthand and transcriptions, that when you get used to the work, you will take all the Churchill calls whenever you are on duty.' I could scarcely believe what I was hearing, yet the Colonel was still glaring at me; no glimmer of a smile, so it wasn't a bad joke. And then to make his point as I reeled out of the door, he shouted after me: 'And you are NOT to take private notes, you are NOT allowed to keep a diary, and you will take NO written material of any kind from this building.' So I didn't.

Bill Fiske, on the other hand, was the complete opposite to the lean and austere Colonel. In his mid-thirties and unfit for military service because of a heart condition, he resembled a young and cherubic Robert Morley. Ever cheerful, his unflappable personality brought us through assorted dramas and crises for the next three and a half years. He had been a businessman during his civilian existence and he soon organised the working life of the Department down to the last detail. I came to realise that the Colonel wasted very few words talking to his troops, and my co-censors – about eight of us – relied on Bill's common-sense approach to high-level security work. Instructions, rules and complaints filtered down to us through Bill, and it was he who listened patiently to our problems, discussed the inevitable post-mortems on past conversations and relayed to us the latest briefings.

'Briefings' is the appropriate word for the scraps of information fed to us by our lords and masters. 'The Need to Know' system was taken to extremes, we thought. 'Tell them as little as possible' seems to have been the Security Chiefs' motto and they obviously had the full agreement of our Colonel. 'Don't encourage them to ask too many questions,' the Colonel concurred. Certainly his own very private character contributed to the pervading mood of secrecy, and I once heard him remark proudly that if a German spy wandered into our office, there would be no apparent clue to the real nature of our work nor the vital role played by our Department in the field of wartime communications.

We worked to an absolute and rigid routine where no exceptions, no alterations were tolerated. This was the only work style that would ensure that the office administration aspect of the security regulations were never breached, and no discretionary powers were given to the censors in respect of the rules and we knew better than to bend them.

We took our responsibilities very seriously indeed. From my days in the Postal Censorship, I had been constantly told that the enemy were adept at piecing together seemingly disconnected bits of information using a library of material they could turn to their advantage. If indeed they had broken the A3 Scrambler, it would not take them long to realise the calibre of the speakers and they would expect an equally high quality of information from this source.

'No call should be listened to casually,' instructed the Colonel. 'Try to anticipate the words and ideas behind the conversation and act swiftly and decisively.' Not so easy when you are scribbling away at high-speed shorthand.

In January 1942, the staff of the Transatlantic Radio Department started to assemble to form a twenty-four-hour, round-the-clock service. From this distance in time, I can understand the Colonel's dismay when confronting this odd and disparate collection of recruits; all eight of us were supposed to be shorthand writers, but it transpired that only I and two other girls could reach a respectable speed. We were about as different from an Indian Army Battalion as you can get.

The men, of course, were over military age, the women younger and from mixed backgrounds. I don't think the Personnel Department at HQ had the faintest idea of the skills, mental alertness or the shorthand speeds that were essential for the job. I was the only one with security experience and training. One girl, Lilla, did a version of speed writing and got along quite well. So we took the VIP calls. Ideally, journalists would have been most suited to the job but one of the reasons for our large turnover in staff was that we were so poorly paid and married personnel found they couldn't afford to live in London and keep a home going in the country. There was no travel allowance, no canteen, nowhere even to take a cup of tea in Union House, so life was expensive. Over the years I remember a dancer from The Tiller Group at the London Palladium (great fun, but no shorthand), Ella Mary Jacobs, who became a dear friend – a Horn Player, a member of the Scots aristocracy and a couple of professors from Bletchley Park Cipher Unit recovering from illnesses. Most of them ended up in the Irish Section.

Eventually, we settled down into a working group: Diana, Matti, Dorothy, Mrs A., Joan, Sylvia and our two men, Norman (gay) and Michel – a French journalist trapped here with a wife and young children in Vichy France. Both were pleasant and sensible companions and both were terrified of the Colonel and spent as much time as possible in the pub next door. Tragedy was never far from our lives. Lilla's fiancé was killed, her brother seriously injured; another girl was deserted by a Canadian soldier; another nice girl from Liverpool went home quickly because her father was taken prisoner of war.

We were presided over by the Colonel and his sidekick, another very elderly white-haired Lt. Colonel Indian Army (Rtd). I used to wonder if he knew which war he was fighting – he spent a lifetime going up and down the Khyber Pass.

From December 1941 to March 1942, procedures for security were discussed by the War Cabinet, the Wireless Telegraphy Board and the Minister of Information. From the inception of the service, the Prime Minister took an active interest in plans initialling minutes and commenting on policies. He wrote personally to Brendon Bracken that not only did he approve of the proposal that every caller, regardless of status and the number of times he had previously used the service, should receive a verbal warning before starting his conversation, but he, too, would be happy to submit to the regulation. Speakers would receive the warning before they were actually connected to their caller, so in fact, I never heard the American censor warn their parties, I was just assured that similar rules operated in Washington.

A memorandum from Brendan Bracken to Churchill about the Transatlantic Telephone Service, including a handwritten note later added by the Prime Minister. It reads: *Personally I approve of this rule and would be very ready to submit myself to it, provided that after I had been warned I could still go on if I thought it right. Certainly the Swiss and the Swedes would be placed under continuous check. You had better bring it up before the Cabinet. WSC* 16.1.42. (Courtesy of The National Archives, UK.)

This warning was read to each caller including Winston
Churchill, the War Cabinet, Chiefs of the Imperial General
Staff and every person who had permission to use the line:

> The enemy is recording your conversation and will compare it
> with previous information in his possession.
> Great discretion is necessary.
> Any indiscretion will be reported by the Censor to the highest
> authority.

The Canadian Censorship authorities adopted a somewhat
longer and sterner version and included a list of subjects that
must never be mentioned.

The onus for ensuring speakers did not infringe the regulations lay with the censor handling the call, so snap decisions
and instant judgements on the suitability of the subject
being discussed were our responsibility alone. This was the
only practical way to run the service; one could not imagine
asking, say, the Chief of the Imperial General Staff to hold
on while seeking another opinion. What was needed by our
VIPs was discretion, respect for and adherence to the rules
and, in the final analysis, plain common sense. However, if
the speaker did step out of line, the censor would disconnect
the call, warn him of the nature of the indiscretion, ask him
if he wished to continue and if so reconnect him. If a second
disconnection was necessary, the speaker would be asked to
devise a different method of disguising his subject matter and
perhaps make the call when he had given more thought as to
its content.

This was the unwritten but obvious list of 'taboo' subjects
that merited instant disconnection:

No reference to: Military, Naval, Airforce operations, troop movements, sailing dates, lack of equipment and supplies or obvious comment on future Service plans.

No reference to: Home or foreign conference venues either past or future, no obvious reference to a particular person's movements. No direct reference to health, working abilities or habits of prominent personalities. No detailed discussions of diplomatic policies, initiatives either domestic or international.

No reference to: lack of food supplies, recent location and damage by enemy aircraft, no comments on public morale.

Speakers should not identify themselves or their opposite number when starting their talks and avoid reference by name to any other third party. Only authorised speakers to use the line and a third party should not be introduced during a conversation unless the censor had been notified in advance.

Each call had to be pre-booked separately and nobody could just lift the receiver – not even Churchill – and be connected immediately to Washington or Ottawa. Calls were booked by telephone to our Department by officially listed duty officers or secretaries in the ministries, private secretaries of the ministers and adjutants of the service chiefs. If the sponsor's name was not on our list, then Bill refused to book the call.

Our duty officer would make out a small docket naming the two speakers and details of their ministry or embassy and hand it to the censor who would then take responsibility for handling the call. The operator at Faraday Building would ring through telling me the call could go ahead, and if I was not ready, then the speakers had to wait till I was, but obviously I didn't dare keep my clients waiting. When I had assembled the tools of my trade, that is, positioned the small switch panel in front of me (depressing its key instantly severed the line), put on my heavy pair of earphones, lined up at least six sharp pencils (no pens allowed), and a high pile of scrap paper, then work could commence.

That paper was the bane of my life. It was roughly A4 size, unlined, a dirty white colour, thick, coarse and totally unsuitable for speed shorthand writing. So, I cut it in half width-ways, drew a line vertically down the middle, the conversation of the London speaker was always written on the left-hand side, the Washington or Ottawa speaker on the right. In that way, I never muddled my speakers and could always attribute 'who said what' later. Our constant pleas for more suitable paper seemed to fall on deaf ears. At least I did not have to spend my spare time drawing lines on the paper as my colleagues had to, for Pitmans shorthand is far easier to write and transcribe quickly when written above and below the lines.

At the end of a long conversation, I could end up with a 3-inch stack of notes that then had to be transcribed into longhand, finally handing in a considerable pile of paper to Bill who put an elastic band round them, attached the docket to the front and handed them in to the Colonel. Heaven knows what he did with them. I knew that a Civil Service messenger appeared every few hours and presumably took them away – but where to? Much later in my career, I plucked up the courage and asked the Colonel where our notes went; I was rewarded with an icy glare – and dead silence. So I never did find out.

The time lapse with the States and Canada dominated our working hours. There were very few calls between 9am and 4pm and only one day shift each was worked on our weekly timetable. Mostly our team of eight censors worked a duty from 4pm to around 11pm, or midnight, or whenever we finished transcribing calls (no work to be left over till the following day) and one all-night duty weekly. We had one day off in eight. My own sleeping clock never really adjusted to this routine and what with a perpetual lack of sleep and our unventilated airless office, I went through the War permanently puss-eyed. It was when working the all-night shift that the Colonel's army camp bed plus blanket came into its own. We were allowed to have a nap on it if there was no work to do and, as a grand gesture, were allowed to boil up his kettle on the gas ring to make a cup of tea – a privilege denied us during daytime working hours.

In the early part of 1942 I was comparatively inexperienced, so when I eventually got to bed, I was too overcome with doubt for sleep to come easily. I would remember every detail of those conversations I had listened to earlier in the evening: had I let pass something vitally important; was that minister whose call I had interrupted twice been justified in speaking so sharply? It took me months to learn how to relax, reassuring myself that a timely intervention on my part, though resented by the caller, could cost valuable lives. The Colonel had no sympathy whatsoever with erring speakers and encouraged us to be ruthless if in doubt and with time I became more confident in justifying my reasons to indiscreet callers and emphasising the need for caution.

Disconnecting a call needed not only instant reaction from the censor and a certain intuitive sense when danger lurked ahead, but manual dexterity as well. With my right hand I depressed the switch key, with the left I had to knock the earphone from my left ear (usually knocking the whole contraption round my neck), grab the earpiece from the nearby telephone and speak to the caller. Connection was merely a matter of raising the switch key and telling the caller to resume his conversation. If I had reason to disconnect a call the second time, I would advise him to abandon it and return when he had devised a safer method of reference.

A minute from Brendan Bracken outlined the procedures agreed by us and the American Censorship authorities harmonising the arrangements that would apply to all the calls. President Roosevelt had approved them and the same censorship routines would apply to his wartime Administration, including Harry Hopkins, War Department personnel, and the London Embassy in Grosvenor Square.

Hedged in by so many restrictions how, one might ask, could anybody conduct a meaningful and intelligent conversation? It was a problem that exercised the minds of the War Cabinet right down to us trying to get some regular ruling on the question. Obviously, nobody could speak endlessly in code, but some method of disguising the subject matter had to be devised.

Finally, on 16 March 1942, the matter was raised again at a meeting of the War Cabinet when they discussed a memorandum written by the chairman of The Wireless Telegraphy Board who suggested a solution. Sir Edward Bridges, secretary to the Cabinet, was always particularly concerned with security leaks and indiscretions and added his own ideas.

The Chief of the Wireless Telegraphy Board outlined a method whereby the Radio Telephone could be used safely and to advantage. Whenever possible, callers should arrange with each other by signal the time and date of their proposed conversation. They should also telegraph in cipher a memorandum written in short numbered paragraphs and then conduct the conversation by referring only to these numbered paragraphs, never revealing the subject matter. Sir Edward Bridges also came up with an idea that would not endanger cipher security and telegrams were always endorsed by the originator 'Re-Cipher in one Timetable'.

At last ground rules were laid down on 25 March 1942. Mr A.S. Hodge of the Ministry of Information was told of the Prime Minister's approval. All very proper and correct, but it took no account at all of the varied personalities using the service, who ranged from the monosyllabic to the extremely verbose.

# 5

# THE BRITISH AND THE VIPS

Before being allowed to handle the calls from senior War Cabinet ministers and the CIGS, I was put to work on what was considered to be 'the B team'. These consisted of calls to and from the various supply ministries, such as Aircraft Production, Food and Transport, talking to our staff in the Washington Embassy, British Purchasing Mission and American colleagues. On the whole, these calls were rather dull, made by top-ranking civil servants who obediently followed the rules, had assembled the correct papers in front of them and generally behaved in an exemplary fashion.

Early in 1942, our military position was dire, and our very existence depended on Lend Lease supplies getting through to us. For us to carry on the War effectively, it was imperative that the deliveries of weapons, fuel, food, ships − anything you care to think of − were shipped over the Atlantic as quickly as possible. This entailed a great deal of organisation and continual discussion as to the means of shipping it across the Atlantic.

Most outstanding in my memory were the conversations made by the civil servants at the Ministry of War Transport. They spoke frequently; two or three times a day was quite normal. Not only did they refer to their own numbered paragraphed memoranda in an enigmatic style, but on top of that, they imposed a code of their own. This consisted of giving particular categories of supplies, shipping data and convoy arrangements domestic names. I was perpetually amazed by the fluency of the speakers who never hesitated in their speech and never laughed at the general dottiness of their conversation. Whoever made up that code must have had quite a sense of humour, so for one week they would chat happily away about 'babies' bottoms' and 'planks of wood', while the following week the code would change and talk would be about 'elephants' trunks, electric light bulbs and vases of flowers'. The buzz words were regularly changed and rarely repeated, and when I once queried if the code was 'safe', I was told 'indeed it was', it had originated from the highest quarter.

All I know is that I never had cause to interrupt their calls and they became part of our working lives, speaking their own special language till the War ended. We realised the importance of the content and never resented their length and, it must be confessed, the sometime tedium, but really they were the perfect conversationalists. I couldn't understand a word of what they were on about and neither, I supposed, could the Germans.

There was a young civil servant, an assistant secretary at the Board of Trade, whose calls I always welcomed. He was an orderly man with his papers ready beforehand (not a condition for high office, I found out); his remarks and replies were brief and to the point and he understood the meaning of security.

His name was Harold Wilson, in his first Government post after leaving Oxford.

I soon came to realise it was not just high office or the urgency of the matter under discussion that made callers careless, it was the nature of their own personality. The more expansive and gregarious the character, the more likely it was that slips of the tongue could occur, not because they deliberately ignored the rules, but their natural conversational style just rose to the surface. One such was Robert Boothby, an ebullient personality and a real character. I was sorry when he left the Cabinet but I was never quite sure what he would say next. Entertaining and witty, he nevertheless made me twitchy.

The same could be said of Lord Beaverbrook, Max Aitkin. He was officially Minister of Supply, a close friend of Churchill, who would send him on frequent visits to Washington and Ottawa when there was an urgent need for an assessment of policy and quick decisions had to be taken. He would phone back his reading of the situation, very often not having sent on his signalled memoranda and it was very difficult, even fearsome, trying to make characters like them tow the line. While Robert Boothby apologised profusely and politely and quite understood the reason for the interruption to his conversation, Lord Beaverbrook could be quite sharp and resented the interference. Nevertheless, one pressed on despite the inference that I made up security regulations expressly for his inconvenience.

I could have told the world long before it was generally known that Clement Attlee was a man of very few words. Unlike many of our speakers who did ramble on a bit (making my writing arm ache somewhat), Mr Attlee's calls, usually to our Washington Embassy, consisted of a few terse sentences that related only to the numbered paragraphs on his papers. I could never form any opinion of his personality as such because he never spoke long enough for me to form a judgement. Nevertheless, he was high up on my list of favourite speakers because of his brevity.

In my personal life, I had never spoken to anybody higher in military rank than a 2nd Lieutenant (my fiancé). Then to be suddenly confronted with a Field Marshal, an Air Chief Marshal and an Admiral of the Fleet was a daunting experience. The Chiefs of the Imperial General Staff, their staff and advisors used the service regularly, linking up with their American opposite numbers and our own military staff in the Washington Embassy, where Field Marshal Sir John Dill was our Chief of Staff and in regular touch with colleagues here. By 1942, high-ranking American Generals and their staff were in constant touch with their London embassy and our Chiefs. General Marshall was a regular user of the service as Land Lease arrangements fell within his orbit of responsibility. Obviously, as these distinguished officers were probably consulted and most certainly agreed to our rules, they were treated with the greatest respect and I seem to remember they dealt with their paperwork with the military precision you would expect.

I remember Air Chief Marshal Sir Charles Portal well, a mild-mannered man whose voice had a boyish quality and seemed to me to be young for such high office. But of all the Service Chiefs – including Lord Mountbatten when he was Chief of Combined Operations – I recall most vividly, my lasting memory is of Field Marshal Lord Alanbrooke.

I thought him a charming, modest and unassuming man, often driven by his lord and master to the edge of exhaustion and exasperation. Of course, anybody intimately connected with Churchill's work style ended up in that condition, and the strain of year after year of working very late nights, very little sleep coupled with enormous responsibilities, appeared to be reflected in his voice. This softly spoken man seemed to be the very antithesis of some of the American top brass who would bark down the phone and who would probably read all the wrong signs into his character for, in reality, he was an extremely tough man. Not till I read his biography by General Sir David Fraser did I come to realise the extent of his influence on Churchill. The Field Marshal accompanied Churchill on all his foreign journeys and if I didn't hear from both of them for a period of time, I deducted they were both away from Downing Street. On the other hand, if Sir Charles Wilson (Churchill's doctor and later Lord Moran) came on the phone, as he frequently did when making personal arrangements for the Prime Minister's trips, and there was silence from his boss, then I assumed he was ill for the doctor always travelled with him. I made this point to the Colonel for I thought if I could make such a deduction, so could the Germans. Lord Moran then did his best to mask his identity if he used the line when Churchill was indisposed.

Within a couple of months working in the Department I found my social life had dwindled to non-existent. My fiancé had sailed off from Greenock at the end of 1941 to an unidentified destination, and I found it just too awkward to explain to casual acquaintances – and friends for that matter – that I worked unsocial hours in an extremely top-secret department. I realised that most people liked a little more elaboration than I was able to supply. But anyway, by the middle of 1942 the workload had become increasingly demanding and I found my entire life revolving round Union House.

I went to the cinema and theatre on my nights off and remember well going to the first Promenade Concerts in the Albert Hall in 1942. Performances used to start around six in the evening and with double daylight saving, I could get home before it was dark. My Great Aunt Isobel was married to Uncle 'A' Hess, the uncle of Myra Hess, and he used to get me tickets for her National Gallery lunchtime concerts; Ella-Mary Jacob (a Union House friend) and we sat on the steps one warm summer day and dreamt of peace. Cousin Myra – as I knew her – was a large, jolly lady and her serious stage presence combined with her divine interpretation of Bach belied her real 'at home nature'.

Writers far more gifted than me have written most movingly about working in wartime London and I cannot compete with their imaginative pens, but it seemed to me I was living on the edge of an unreal world. Union House, Armour House, the pub and the little church on the corner of Gresham Street had survived the Blitz, then absolute devastation as far as the eye could see. Summer brought pink campion and wild flowers growing strongly amongst the ruins and it was peaceful to eat my sandwiches there before returning to listen to more disembodied voices.

The Blackout was a bore but part of wartime life, though those journeys home from work around midnight remain fresh in my mind even today. I caught the Underground from St Paul's Station to West Hampstead changing onto the Bakerloo Line at Oxford Circus. I read recently somewhere that those sheltering in the Underground had a wonderful time with parties, knees-ups, canteens and fun all round. Maybe they did – sometimes. True there was a unique feeling of comradeship amongst the shelterers and a deep sense of community but I remember the hardships, the sheer effort of just trying to survive. All around us we had Free French, Free Poles, Dutch, Norwegian, Czech and, of course, American servicemen, but Free Englishmen were hard to find. They were serving in the Forces all over the world, leaving the responsibility of bringing up a family and earning a wage to implement their not excessive Forces' pay to the women.

Being a regular at Oxford Circus station and standing at the same spot waiting for the Stanmore train, I got friendly with a family who came from the East End every night because, they claimed, one more good shake from a bomb would bring their battered house down on their heads. The family consisted of Grandma, her sister (whose husband was killed in the First World War), Grandma's daughter Rose, and her two boys – back from being evacuated in the country because they hated it there, aged about eight and ten. Rose's husband was serving in the 8th Army as my fiancé was and we used to complain about the scarcity of their letters.

Those two boys were the fastest sprinters among a gang of kids who used to scamper round the labyrinth of passages that honeycomb Oxford Circus station. If I missed my train, I would have a wait of around twenty minutes for the next, so Rose would recruit me and any American soldier also on the platform to join in the hunt for the runaways and bribe them out of hiding with their chocolate bars. Trying to get children to sleep before the trains stopped running was impossible if their pitch was on the platform, where it was considered to be cooler from the draught coming from the tunnel than in the connecting passages around the station. Rose and Auntie did office cleaning near Oxford Street starting early morning while Grandma took the boys home and got them ready for school. Rose also did a part-time factory shift; I thought it was a hard life indeed and admired their cheerfulness and good humour.

Listening as I did night after night to men in high office accepting their responsibilities as a matter of course, and the privileges too that accompany that role, I could not help but wonder if they felt but the most academic understanding of the life of ordinary poor people, the hardships war had inflicted on them together with the sadness and the worry of separation from loved ones. The shelter folk adored the Royal Family and believed they truly cared; they loved and trusted 'Winnie' implicitly to see them through to victory, and they had faith in 'Monty' and 'Ike' to win the battles, but they seemed to have little interest in any other politician except perhaps those on the LCC (London County Council).

To those women in Oxford Street station one thing was very clear, they vowed they would not go back to the bad old days; things were going to change. After all, 'that's what we are fighting for'. I wondered if those elderly pre-war politicians had any idea of the undercurrent of strong feelings people in the shelters, and for that matter I supposed in the rest of the country, harboured towards their leaders.

Christmas was a perfunctory celebration. The line closed on Christmas Eve only opening up again at 4pm on Christmas Day. Most of my colleagues lived out of London and travelled home for the short break, and as few calls were expected, I did the duty rota alone. I had an excellent Christmas routine and my three years in the Department were spent exactly the same way.

My mother's cousins, Fred and Clarissa Davidson, took a suite at the Dorchester Hotel for Christmas and invited my mother and me for Christmas lunch. The cousins were twins, then into their seventies and greatly involved in music, musicians and the arts and their guests reflected their tastes. Over the years I had met Isaac Stern, Ida Haendal and once I had the thrill of sitting next to Marjorie Hammond, the great Australian singer whom I had heard many times on the radio, admiring her voice enormously. I dearly wanted to discuss opera while she was intent only on talking about her golf handicap. The Dorchester kitchens pulled out all the stops and provided a quite splendid traditional Christmas lunch: turkey, trimmings, puddings, the lot – quite an achievement in food-rationing days.

After lunch, we would return to the sitting room to listen to the King's wireless broadcast and then a taxi would be ordered to take me to work. Clarissa told the kitchen that her young cousin was on 'Hush-Hush' work, and they provided me with sufficient food and drink to keep me going for twenty-four hours. There were all sorts of rarities in those parcels including proper white flour rolls, an orange, a bottle of wine, and at 4pm I would batten down the hatches and wait for Bill to come in around midday on Boxing Day. I still say a mental 'thank you' to the Dorchester as I pass by for cheering up my Christmas shift.

I would hope my favourite speakers would wish to talk to each other. The Dutch royal family were the only reminder I ever had during my working life that the sadness of separation could affect the highest in the land as equally as the shelter folk in Oxford Circus station. Queen Wilhelmina and Prince Bernard lived in this country while Princess Juliana with their four small daughters lived in Canada. The Queen missed her grandchildren very much indeed as did their Papa, especially at Christmas when these telephone calls meant a very great deal to them. The Queen would talk first to her daughter, at that time the family were much concerned about the partial-sightedness of the youngest little girl; then the three older girls would come to the telephone to talk first to their grandmother and then to their father. Princess Beatrix was a delight – a real little chatterbox – talking away in excellent English saying how much she enjoyed her Canadian school but how she missed her Papa and grandmother. Her sisters were too shy, their English too halting the first year I heard them, but by the end of their Canadian stay, all of them were speaking fluently. I thought this a call I should not have to listen to and just wrote 'personal' in my transcription.

King Frederick of Denmark, and King Haakon of Norway also spoke to their families in America from time to time. Exile made great demands on their emotions, and their manner and speech was subdued and restrained.

As far as I know, our own royalty never used the TRS. There was a rumour that the King wished to speak to Mrs Roosevelt after the President's death, but I don't believe the call materialised.

Apart from Queen Wilhelmina and Princess Juliana, the only other woman to use our service was Madam Chang Kaichek, wife of the Chinese Nationalist leader who was living here. Occasionally she would speak briefly to other Chinese nationals in Washington on ordinary routine matters.

Being such a secret department had serious practical drawbacks. Nobody – that is no other Government Department in the vicinity, and there were various branches of the Post Office nearby – had ever heard of us and so had absolutely no idea of our work; nobody therefore wanted to feed us. It seemed the Colonel hadn't realised we might need something to eat during our evening shifts; he made no arrangements, just leaving us to fend for ourselves. The men used to take a liquid supper break at the pub next door, but Lilla, Joan Beard and I liked something to eat and some fresh air to go with it.

The choice was hardly extensive. First, there was Diviani's, an Italian restaurant just about functioning amid the ruins of Newgate Street, which stayed open till 7pm and was staffed by two very elderly and decrepit waiters. The large knotted veins in their bald heads were visible as they tottered out of the kitchen clutching one plate of spaghetti at a time and would take another five minutes at least to eventually reappear with the parmesan cheese. We would spend the time speculating on whether such an energetic undertaking as serving our dinner would hasten their demise and so we decided to take our custom elsewhere. Many years later, I read a most amusing account written by Tom Hulton (in his memoirs, I believe) of the aged staff in Manzoni's in Fetter Lane. My lot were their grandfathers.

So we decided to give the Post Office workers' canteen in King Edward Building a try. We were greeted suspiciously when we told how we came from Union House and we were told to go to a small table right at the end of a large, busy canteen full of hungry postal workers. All I ever remember eating there were semi-cold sausages; nobody spoke to us, and obviously nobody had filled in the right indent forms allowing for our rations. We were not welcome.

'Staff Welfare' was not a concept understood by our Colonel, but we pleaded with him to make some arrangements. Finally the staff canteen in Faraday Building agreed to take us in where the food was really very good, the vegetable dishes quite excellent. Its only drawback was that it was about five minutes' walk away and not too healthy when the A.A. guns were blazing away. Once I had to side-step very smartly into the ruins of Nicholson's in St Paul's churchyard when a large piece of shrapnel whizzed by, and I developed quite a good sprinting speed across the precinct during the V1 attacks.

Now, when I see that stylised wartime poster of the dome of St Paul's Cathedral illuminated by searchlights, I remember the real thing, searchlights sweeping the sky, St Paul's silhouetted in their bright light and the rumble of distant gunfire.

I had come from a family of Winston Churchill watchers. Every step in his political career, his chances of again reaching high office, his speeches and events in his family life were carefully noted and discussed at length around our dining table.

Why though? Well, my mother's family had political links and even enjoyed the friendship of the Great Man. My maternal grandmother came from Manchester where her much older brother, Dr Joseph Dulberg, was a medical doctor with a practice in the poorest area of the city, a kindly philanthropic man whose liberal views were converted into political practice. He was an enthusiastic member of the Liberal Party and when Churchill became a member for Oldham, Uncle Joe became his agent and worked again on his behalf at the By-Election in northwest Manchester, which Churchill had to fight after his elevation to the Cabinet in 1904 – a parliamentary procedure long abandoned.

Churchill failed to gain the northwest Manchester seat because, he claimed, of the bitter opposition of the Jewish community to certain sections of the Aliens Act. Uncle Joe became secretary of a committee consisting of prominent Jewish communal leaders aimed at keeping the public informed about the stages of the fight against discriminatory clauses in the Bill. When Churchill was re-elected, he reflected their views in Parliament to great effect and eventually, the Bill in that particular form was dropped by the Balfour Government.

So it seemed that the natural thing to do was to invite Uncle Joe to his wedding at St Margaret's Church, Westminster.

A letter from Ruth's Great Uncle Dr Joseph Dulberg to Winston Churchill, written in 1907.

A second letter from Dr Joseph Dulberg to Winston Churchill, congratulating him on the announcement of his engagement in 1908.

Apparently this threw the family into something of a dilemma; it seems that Uncle Joe's wife, Auntie Hannah, was far too eccentric and unconventional to be taken into polite society, so my mother, then aged twenty-four, was selected to accompany her uncle to the nuptials of Miss Clementine Hosier and Mr W.S. Churchill.

This event made an enormous impression on my mother, who for years after would tell me about the beautiful bride, the handsome groom and details of the dress mother made for herself, to say nothing of the enormous hat she and her sister constructed out of flowers, bird feathers and tulle. Thereafter, she took the greatest interest in Churchill's career culminating in absolute hero-worship when he became Prime Minister. It was surely an ironic twist of fate that now she could not mention – even to her closest friends – how I too had become associated with her hero.

Somewhat naively, I suppose, I imagined I was going to hear Churchill speak on the telephone rather in the same style as he spoke on the radio. That magnificent oratory, those stirring sentiments would ring in my ears, my shorthand would be more than equal to record the fluency and eloquence of our leader's language, and I waited for my first call with a mixture of pride and nervousness for what I just knew would be the most uplifting experience of a lifetime. I could not have been more wrong.

One night, after about a fortnight of working my passage and getting to know the routines, Bill quite casually handed me the usual docket with the speakers' names on it. I looked – I had never heard of a 'Mr White' wanting to speak to a 'Mr Smith'.

I said, 'Who on earth is ...', but the Faraday operator's bell rang telling me my speakers were on the line ready to start their conversation, so I never heard Bill's answer, only saw him grin. In the middle of the little 'warning' speech, a very well-known voice indeed roared down the line telling me in no uncertain manner to hurry up. I faded ... very quickly indeed. The easily recognisable drawl of Mr Smith answered immediately.

I don't know whose bright idea it was to make Churchill and President Roosevelt speak under the *nom des plumes* of Mr White and Mr Smith, but I should have thought even the stupidest German would have recognised their voices and the great men themselves thought it rather a joke.

'Is that you, Mr Smith?'
'How are you, Mr White, and how is the Colonel?'

The Colonel? Which Colonel? 'The Colonel' turned out to be Mrs Churchill. Similar expressions of good will from 'Mr White'.

Then the hard talk began. I was completely entranced listening to their informal conversation and subsequent business discussion, sitting there with a stupid smile on my face, quite incapable of writing down anything. My Colonel was not pleased.

I did not do much better on the next calls either. Intense nervousness as to my reception coupled with disbelief at my own situation seemed to freeze my right hand and it took several calls before I could concentrate completely on its contents. 'Mr White' would sometimes become 'John Martin' (his Principal Private Secretary), or Colonel Warden and I was never absolutely sure who was to be the voice behind the name.

In those early 1942 talks with the President, when the news from the war fronts was grim and depressing, when our losses in Africa and the fall of Singapore was matched by American unpreparedness of the Japanese attacks and the loss of their Pacific bases, Churchill's tone of voice was always strong, confident and had no doubts whatsoever when speaking on the phone about our ultimate victory. He certainly 'sold' our determination to triumph to a not-so-certain President. Before settling down to their paperwork, there was always a little informal chat. They would refer very obliquely to points made in their numerous letters to each other and Churchill would sometimes describe the excellent dinner he had just eaten to a somewhat surprised President. I got the impression that the President was never quite sure what our Prime Minister would say next (neither did I for that matter), with the result that often his responses were slow and lacked the spontaneity of his opposite number.

Churchill used to end his conversations with a phrase that I simply could not understand. I didn't think it could possibly be a coded message to the President, but I had got into such severe trouble from the Colonel for not handing in completed transcriptions, that every time Churchill said what I thought sounded like 'KBO', I wrote down KBO too – carefully in shorthand, then Kay Be O in my longhand transcription.

After a few such calls, the Colonel approached.

'No need to write down KBO every time. Don't you know what it means?'

'No, Sir.'

'KBO means Keep Buggering On.'

Straight-backed and straight-faced, the Colonel strode off.

I used to think I was not the only one who didn't understand what those initials meant, for the President never made any response whatsoever to Churchill's special form of farewell.

I got the impression that he enjoyed the *Boys' Own Paper* style of disguising the true subject matter, for sometimes his conversation became so enigmatic that I didn't think the other speaker understood the references. He certainly exploited his weakness for mispronouncing people's names. Hidden in all the verbiage one night came the word 'OOO-SHAY', spoken with the accent on the first syllable. That 'OOO-SHAY' = 'OOO-JAY' = UJ = UNCLE JOE = Stalin. I didn't have the nerve to interrupt him to remind him of the rule of no direct allusion to highly placed personalities – anyway, it took me a minute to connect. It took me a minute too to realise that when he talked about 'God Almighty in the North' he was referring to Sir Stafford Crips, our then ambassador in Moscow, and definitely *not* one of Churchill's favourites because of his non-drinking and smoking habits, though he respected his talents as an able diplomat and administrator.

The Prime Minister constantly changed his personality according to whom he was talking. To President Roosevelt he was his personal friend, his equal, conversation flowed pleasantly along and the bond of friendship between them was apparent.

To our ambassador in Washington, Lord Halifax, he was polite and formal, and talk was confined solely to signal and memorandum matters. Yet here again, whilst recognising his diplomatic skill, he remembered the role he had played in the Chamberlain Government and did not wish to become too closely associated with a minister who had played a big part in pre-war appeasement policies.

That well-documented habit of the Prime Minister sending enquiring signals requesting information and expecting the reply yesterday extended to our staff in Washington. Once, very late at night, I heard him absolutely wipe the floor with a young wretched officer who had not answered his signal sent the previous week. I was really sorry for the chap squirming under such an onslaught.

I know much has been written about Churchill's wartime lifestyle that for me to describe it again would seem unnecessarily repetitive, but his daily routine influenced our working day and the life of the Department.

The working day would begin at 8am when Churchill would breakfast. A work period would follow, probably attending a Cabinet meeting in the Great George Cabinet Rooms. After 1941, when the Debating Chamber of the House of Commons had been badly damaged by enemy bombs, with the object of finishing its business before dark, the Commons changed its working timetable. Instead of sessions starting at 2.45pm, as was the practice in peace time, sittings started at 11.30am and Churchill wished, whenever possible, to be in the House for Question Time. In fact, parliamentary sittings were regularly altered as a precaution against enemy action.

After an excellent lunch, Churchill would depart to bed for his afternoon nap, rising around 5pm, just around the time when it was practical to start phoning Washington and Ottawa;

then more work till dinner, which appeared to be the highlight of his working day. Being naturally sociable and gregarious, this was the part of the day he enjoyed most when his family, staff, friends and visiting statesmen joined him round the dinner table. I was constantly surprised at the importance Churchill placed on food and drink, his body metabolism seemed to demand regular replenishments of both and he would often describe the excellent dinner and fine wine he had enjoyed. I also heard him mention gratefully the presents he had received from friends and well-wishers: 'a fine pair of grouse' and 'a side of Welsh Lamb' went down very well.

At dinner he would drink a bottle of champagne, washed down with brandy, and then sipping weak whisky and water, his working day would last till about 2–3am and all his exhausted staff would be in attendance (including a censor from the Radio Department).

He enjoyed working in bed from where he would make his late-night calls, sounds of paper rustling in the background. Moods varied considerably, exuding bonhomie and goodwill to the President right through the scale to the most sarcastic and withering of comments. It was not till after the War, when Churchill admitted to his 'Black Dog Days' that I realised their significance. These were the days when deep depression over-took him, when even the briefest of conversations was a supreme effort, his speech so laboured, and the pauses in between so long that I could easily record his conversation in longhand.

I was very, very alarmed. I thought he sounded at the end of his tether and I told Bill that I believed the Prime Minister was either dreadfully ill or completely exhausted, and was it a good idea, I wondered, for security reasons, whether he should speak on an open line. Nobody told me that these bouts of depression were just another facet of his personality (I don't suppose the Colonel knew either), and I was very distressed to hear the great man so troubled. Within a few days he had recovered, speech returned, good humour blended with a certain irascibility – we were back on course.

An 'after a good dinner' call between Churchill and Lord Beaverbrook used to set the alarm bells ringing. They were good old friends, comfortably at ease with each other and very often Max – then Minister of Supply – would be sent off to Washington or Ottawa to ascertain certain information and he would report back to the boss. Neither ever offended, in my hearing anyway, and Max would be on his best behaviour then.

When all the late-night calls from the Ministries and the Cabinet Office had finished and every sensible person had gone to bed, I would get a call booked in from a 'Mr White' or John Martin who wanted a chat with his old friend Bernard Baruch. They had known each other a long time, their friendship reaching back for many years, long before Churchill had attained high office. Bernie had shown the Churchill family great kindness during the Depression Years and they had kept in close touch ever since, especially as Bernie now appeared to be writing some sort of global report and wanted his old friend's opinion. It seemed to me that when too many chapters sent along by Bernie piled up in the 'In Tray', the Prime Minister's conscience would prompt him to phone him up for an encouraging little chat. Then, I thought, they were two nice old gentlemen talking of this and that and I could well imagine Churchill sitting in bed sipping his whisky and Bernard Baruch probably doing the same thing.

In 1942, we had a radio telephone line operating to Cairo. At that time, Harold Macmillan was Minister of State in the Middle East and General Sir Harold Alexander was our Commander in Chief at GHQ. Again, it was thought to be essential to have a verbal link operating between London and Cairo in view of the importance of that theatre of war. But unlike the line to Washington where the reception was good if sometimes a little faint, the Cairo line was extremely noisy, and Mr Macmillan sounded as if he was speaking in the middle of the desert in a severe sandstorm. He would shout his greetings to Churchill who had little patience with an atmospheric telephone line and after a few seconds would slam down the receiver muttering 'I can't hear a bloody word', leaving Mr Macmillan still trying to make himself heard above the crackle. Anthony Eden did his best with the Cairo calls, plodding on trying to get Harold Macmillan to hear, but the line was too poor to hold an intelligent conversation, and was eventually abandoned.

In my civilian days, I always imagined Anthony Eden to possess a rather debonair and jaunty personality – perhaps it was the hat that gave that impression, but in reality, I found him to be a very serious and somewhat humourless man. He used the line extensively, making numerous and almost daily calls to Washington and Ottawa, and when on his travels, would report regularly back to Churchill whom he would refer to as 'The Captain'. He seemed devoted to him, and the Captain was always happy to hear his voice (not so with some of his other callers).

It takes two to make a telephone call, one on each side of the Atlantic, so now to introduce the other characters in the partnership: our American allies.

# 6

# THE AMERICANS AND CANADIANS

## The Americans

Our Post Office had been in contact with the American Telephone and Telegraph Company as early as January 1940, setting out interim proposals for censorship on the Radio Telegraphy channels. The AT&T Co. handled the Washington Terminal and the American Censorship authorities synchronised the security rules with our own Postal and Telegraph Censorship on staffing, timetables, etc., and the finer points of coordinating such a service continued until March 1942. There was to be a censor at the Washington terminal and presumably because I never heard her warning the speaker (like our routine, this was done before connection), it was similar in content to the British version. By the time I arrived in the Department, all the technical arrangements were working smoothly, no problems were apparent and calls followed each other in an orderly manner.

The staff at the American Embassy in Grosvenor Square were a cheerful bunch, partly because their diplomatic and consular staff were much younger than our civil servants, they were far more relaxed and informal without the tensions and strains reflected in the voices. Also, I suspect, there was a much more pleasant atmosphere since John Winant, a personal friend of President Roosevelt, had succeeded the gloomy Joseph Kennedy as ambassador. I liked them a lot.

There was Charlie Winthrop Brown and Walter Thayer, whom I remember particularly well for they were resident at the embassy, as well as numerous visitors like Robert Sherwood, Henry Morganthau, Sumner Wells, Edward Stettinus, various politicians both Democrat and Republican parties and a constant stream of Top Brass from General Marshall downwards.

Without exception, they all wanted to phone back home. I came to the conclusion that talking on a phone is part of the American national psyche – they seemed to be born with this instinct to grab a phone if they saw one, it didn't matter if the call was to across the road or across the Atlantic. I used to wonder why they bothered to make all these calls lasting a couple of minutes or so. Perhaps Washington just needed to be reassured that Grosvenor Square and its occupants had survived the night. Eventually 'authority' caught up and put an end to casual chatting, but it must have been beyond belief for them to realise that this was the only phone link with home.

In those early days, because the Americans were so informal, they were what I used to think of as 'word happy'. They were not used to choosing their words carefully and unlike us had not really had to take heed of our national 'Walls Have Ears' campaign. Our Censorship arrangements with our Allies contained an instruction that the British censors should not interrupt a call if the indiscretion is made by the speaker at the Washington end, and we could only control our caller. Consequently I remember about a couple of instances when I did interrupt a call asking

*1* Ruth Ive in the 1940s when she worked in the Postal and Telegraph Censorship

*2* Kurt Vetterlein, the electrical engineer at Valkenswaard who decoded the A3 Scrambler, the code that protected the Transatlantic Telephone Link

*3 (Right)* Armour House, St Martin's Le Grand. This building, next door to the Censorship Department, was damaged by a parachute mine in 1940

*4 (Below)* Union House, the Postal and Telegraph Censorship Department headquarters, survived the Blitz and is here photographed in the 1980s

POSTAL & TELEGRAPH CENSORSHIP DEPARTMENT,

Union House,

St. Martin's-le-Grand,

E.C.1.

Ref: AGLC/CML

14th July, 1945.

To whom it may concern.

### MISS RUTH MAGNUS

Miss Magnus joined this Department on 14th September, 1942. Since then she has worked almost the whole time under my personal supervision.

She was picked out for highly skilled and confidential work on the Transatlantic Radio Telephone Service. Recently she was chosen as the best Censor out of nearly 150 employed here.

Miss Magnus is a first class stenographer.

She is highly recommended for work requiring tact and discretion.

ASST. CENSOR

5  Ruth's character reference, provided by her supervisor at Union House

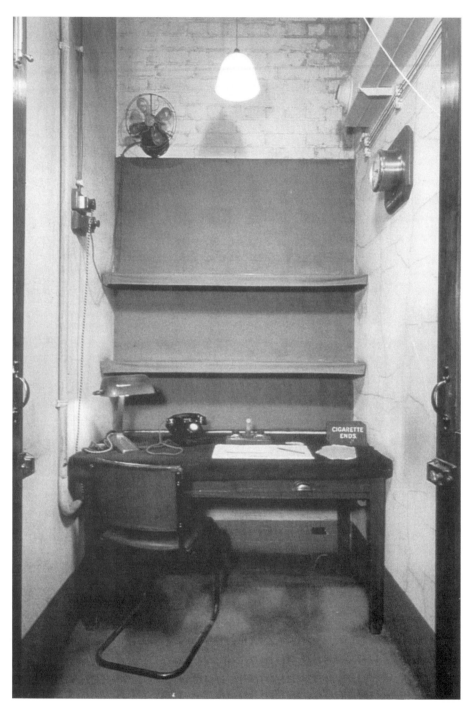

*6* This is the telephone that Churchill used to make his Transatlantic telephone calls. The door to this room displayed a sign that either read 'Vacant' or 'Engaged' in order to disguise the room as a toilet. Image courtesy of Phil Reed of The Churchill Museum

7 Map of Valkenswaard, showing the Bunker in 1945

*8* Valkenswaard today. During the war, this building was used as the German Intelligence Centre, and was disguised to look like a Dutch farmhouse

9 Ruth's cousin Edward Lobel, through whom she secured her first position in the Postal and Telegraph Censorship. He had been recruited in 1939

10 Ruth's husband (right) enjoying the tobacco so kindly supplied throughout the war by Harrods

11 Ruth Ive and Hans Knap in the Amsterdam Hotel

12 Ruth Ive and Randolph Churchill at the Churchill War Rooms

the speaker here not to elicit such direct answers to his queries. But the American censors soon caught on and were as ruthless and quick off the mark as we could wish.

'Mr Smith' was always beyond reproach. The President was ever courteous, polite and affable – to everybody. His manner never varied and he spoke to his ambassador and staff at the embassy in the same equable manner as he did to our Prime Minister. I never remember hearing him raise his voice or express any irritation in any situation. The two leaders had one vocal quality in common – both gave the impression of absolute authority.

I recall one incident very well when, in the middle of what I judged to be an innocuous business conversation, the Washington censor interrupted the call. While I had to assure my somewhat aggrieved speaker that all was well, the President returned to the line moments later resuming the subject in the same even tenor of voice as before. This was the one and only time I actually heard my opposite number; she started to speak to the President before she depressed the disconnection switch. I was delighted to hear her for she sounded very competent and not a bit in awe of her distinguished customer.

I suppose in those early months of 1942, the two leaders spoke several times a week, sometimes for a few minutes just confirming arrival of important papers, other times when more detail was needed for up to, say, fifteen minutes. Both were mindful of the security risk, and apart from that one incident, the censors never had cause to disrupt their talks.

Of all the Americans, Harry Hopkins is the personality I recall with clarity and affection. The first call I took from him was from Churchill; this time he was booked in as 'John Martin' but by now I was used to his various disguises. He and Harry got along famously and had a great rapport going between them.

Harry Hopkins was President Roosevelt's legs, his special representative, his winged envoy for whom he travelled ceaselessly round and round the world. From Washington to London, back to the States, on to Moscow, attending every Summit Conference, it was a punishing lifestyle even for the fittest of men, which Harry certainly was not. On that first call I took, Churchill asked anxiously after his health for he apparently had just come out of hospital having had several blood transfusions. He constantly complained about the lack of efficient central heating here and said he never took off his overcoat in London; he stayed at the embassy but was to be found mostly in the bar at Claridge's Hotel.

Everybody, from the President downwards, enquired after his health. Everybody too asked him if he was taking his pills and General Marshall, the American Chief of Staff who often travelled with Harry, seemed to have the job of seeing that he took them.

In those early days, both Harry Hopkins and General Marshall were responsible for implementing the Lease Lend Act and smoothing out the problems and difficulties that accompanied such a complicated scheme. Harry was constantly on the phone and, I used to think, was something of a high security risk, simply because he was such a relaxed personality. It just didn't come naturally for him to guard his speech.

Out of the many transatlantic calls that he made, only a very few transcriptions have survived. I am including one made in December 1941 before our joint rules were rigidly enforced but it gives some idea as to subject matter discussed and the problems we censors had to contend with.

The context of the call was to reassure Beaverbrook that despite American entry into the War and its own need for military supplies, the shipments scheduled to sail shortly for the Middle East would sail as previously arranged.

BEAVERBROOK: Is that you, Harry?

HOPKINS: Yes.

BEAVERBROOK: Did you get a telegram from Averell; can you help us there?

HOPKINS: I can assure you we can.

BEAVERBROOK: That is very fine.

HOPKINS: And in very important ways. I will not mention details, but it is encouraging and I am going to talk to Morris Wilson and Ed Taylor tonight.

BEAVERBROOK: That is very fine indeed. Thank you.

HOPKINS: Don't worry.

BEAVERBROOK: That is grand.

HOPKINS: In order to make it really tough for Hitler we will undoubtedly increase our amounts.

BEAVERBROOK: I can't hear you.

HOPKINS: We are going to do far better.

(Communication cut at this point and resumed later.)

HOPKINS: Hello Max.

BEAVERBROOK: Yes Harry.

HOPKINS: I wanted to say that we are going to do far better than you or I ever thought. Much better.

BEAVERBROOK: That is very fine.

HOPKINS: If Hitler thought he could start a war and do that, he is going to be greatly mistaken.

BEAVERBROOK: Fine. I will put Averell on to you.

HOPKINS: Hello Ave. Things are going to be alright here.

HARRIMAN: That is fine.

HOPKINS: Don't worry.

HARRIMAN: We are not at all.

HOPKINS: Things are going to turn out far better for you over there in the long run and in the not distant future. They made another mistake by God. Don't worry.

HARRIMAN: I would like to hear from you once in a while.
HOPKINS: You can imagine what is going on here, but you can count on it, we are not going to let them down.
HARRIMAN: All right. Goodbye.
HOPKINS: Goodbye Ave.

Please note that neither of these two gentlemen took the slightest notice of the censor's warnings. They would have been asked not to make direct references to personalities or any immediate event – and in fact be more sensible and reticent on what they knew well to be an open telephone line with the Germans listening to their every word.

My Colonel, quite rightly, would have been furious and aghast if I had handed in such a transcription, and it was no wonder that the Chairman of the Wireless Telegraphy Board was seriously perturbed by this example – and others – of potential leaks of top-secret information, and wrote to Sir Edward Bridges of their concern. Sir Edward promptly minuted the Prime Minister, asking him to bring the matter to the attention of the War Cabinet at the next meeting on 16 March 1942, and instruct the ministers to bring his warning to the attention of their staff and themselves.

Our minister, Brendan Bracken, wrote to Churchill telling him that President Roosevelt had given his approval and had made reciprocal arrangements with the American Censorship authorities. As a result of this, Sir Edward Bridges was instructed to write to all the various Government Offices with more dire warnings and could only hope that the American Censorship Department did the same.

By then Harry was controlling the more exuberant side of his nature, and I always looked forward to hearing his humorous and laconic conversational style. I was so intrigued by his personality that I decided I wanted to know what he looked like, so when I heard he had arrived in London, I went off to the Newsreel

Cinema – and there he was, long, lanky, grinning broadly, huddled up in an enormous overcoat, getting off a plane.

The Radio Department always felt a trifle neglected because of the absence of anybody of any status visiting us and taking an interest in our work, apart from Rear Admiral Sir Lionel Sturdee (who our Colonel reported to) putting his head round the door occasionally. Perhaps they didn't tell anybody where we were. On the other hand, we were certainly one of the American tourist sights. Parties of high-ranking brass, five-star generals would arrive, expressing reactions from mild surprise to downright incredulity and amazement at our ancient equipment and Spartan existence. I spent a very pleasant evening with a charming army officer watching me work, a 1940s film star called Tom Brown who cheered me up no end. We had visits from Norwegians, Dutch – but I don't think our minister, Brendan Bracken, ever found his way to Union House.

Obviously, my strongest memory is of Mr White and Mr Smith and the obvious rapport between them. Of course, as the War wound its way onwards, as is well documented, there were areas of disagreement and dissension over policies, particularly over spheres of interest as in the Mediterranean, but I feel convinced that if it were not for the genuine and mutual admiration they felt for each other, those differences would have led to a souring of the relationship and its subsequent detrimental effect on our joint war effort.

## The Canadians

In Canada the Transatlantic Radio Service was handled by the Bell Telephone Company. They were required to loop their calls from Montreal where the Canadian Censorship

Authorities monitored the calls, and the same security routines were practiced, such as from Canada to British territory in the Caribbean and to Latin America. Consequently they operated a far more international service with censors taking calls in Spanish, Portuguese and French.

The real headache for the Canadians was the telephone link-up between Newfoundland and America, not only during the early days of the War when one would expect teething troubles, but right up until 1944 when our boss, Sir Edwin Herbert, was called in by the Canadian Secretary of State for External Affairs to advise on the continual leak of vital information across the border. At the request of and by agreement with the United States Censorship, such calls were treated as Canadian and to be censored in Montreal.

It seems that though monitoring was conducted both in St John's and Montreal, the staff at the latter were employed by the Canadian Censorship while the St John's monitors were the telephone operators and not specially skilled in monitoring.

It appears that quite a high proportion of calls to America were correctly interrupted and despite local opposition to the imposition of security restrictions to a Censorship routine as used in London, methods had to be used to plug the leaks.

Apart from the Supply Ministries' representatives reporting home, Ottawa became a sort of staging post for War Cabinet ministers and Service Chiefs visiting the States calling in for informal talks with their Canadian counterparts, all of whom seemed to provide a nice relaxing few days away from the War.

The Governor General Rt Hon. Earl of Athlone, a very courtly gentleman usually spoke to Anthony Eden. I personally liked and remember well Malcolm McDonald who was our High Commissioner, but it was those two old friends, Mackenzie King and Churchill who were the stars of this particular line.

# 7

# THE RUSSIANS

Historians can always quote examples when the whole history of mankind might have been changed had it not been for one quite extraordinary event, one coincidence quite beyond world leaders' imagination when planning their grand strategies. Our Russian link from London to Moscow was one such example.

By the spring of 1942, the Department had become very busy indeed, call after call following each other in close succession, some for just a moment or so, others from the Supply Ministries lasting for about twenty minutes. It seemed to be security policy for as few censors as possible to be employed and consequently our team of eight had to work very, very hard for long shifts at a time.

I was living with my mother in Hampstead, working about five shifts weekly from 4pm to around midnight, plus a weekly all-night stint. By the time I had finished my long-hand transcriptions of the calls I had monitored during the evening, placed them on the Colonel's desk and struggled through the sleeping people in the Underground, it was often about 1am before I saw my front door.

The news was grim too. Public demand for a 'Second Front Now' were vociferous, Parliament demanded to know why more aid wasn't being sent to Russia, newspaper headlines, public campaigns and demonstrations of support became everyday news, and everybody wanted to support the Russian people's struggle against Germany.

In fact, both Churchill and Mr Eden wanted to demonstrate our good faith very badly indeed. Churchill was particularly anxious to enhance his reputation by giving practical aid and encouragement to Russia, especially in the light of his forthcoming visit to Moscow. So when Mr Molotov, the Russian Foreign Minister, visited Mr Eden in London in June 1942 asking that the Radio Telephone Link should become operational between Moscow and London, the request was very seriously considered. Mr Molotov told Mr Eden that he would very much appreciate being able to talk to his ambassador in London, Ivan Maisky, and this concession would be well received by Mr Stalin as a gesture of friendship between our two countries.

It seems the matter was raised several times at the Censorship Sub-Committee of the War Cabinet and various considerations influenced their final decision. Most importantly, the Russians themselves were very keen to have the Radio Link extended to Moscow. Our Post Office agreed that this was quite a practical matter and presented no technical difficulties and that, in theory, there was already a line operating from Washington to Moscow; and the Russians themselves would be deeply suspicious if we threw doubts on the efficiency of their security measures. In fact, their security routines and arrangements were probably just as good as ours, and the Committee felt they would be quite unjustified in denying our allies a service that was already available to the Americans.

However, there were some members of the Censorship Sub-Committee who had serious misgivings, believing that practice is very different from theory, and voiced their by-now usual arguments: that it would be quite impossible to avoid the enemy gathering some essential information when the censors themselves had insufficient knowledge of events to make a timely intrusion when speakers were temporarily forgetful.

But finally Mr Churchill himself summed up the whole matter in agreeing to the Russians' request for this 'unsafe' link with London, so long as the security risk was emphasised, that only a certain number of high-ranking personnel be permitted to speak and that our Department should recruit a number of 'intelligent fluent Russian-speaking Englishmen as Censors'.

Then in October 1942, the Foreign Office spiked the whole argument by informing Churchill that a service between Moscow and Washington routed through London was to become operational, so London reservations became academic and the link became official.

At ground level, little bits of information, various rumours and gossip filtered down to us over the months till the news finally broke that we were to have a new recruit, a fluent Russian-speaking, shorthand-writing Englishman. I envisaged a handsome White Russian émigré who had somehow managed to become naturalised while attending commercial school to learn shorthand, an always helpful individual who would help us out with 'the babies' bottoms brigade'. We were told with great seriousness by our Personnel Department that fluent Russian-speaking, shorthand-writing Englishmen were rather thin on the ground and would take some finding – and of course, such a person would be subject to the strictest security vetting. 'But of course,' we said, and waited … and waited.

Eventually, a short, middle-aged balding man turned up one morning and announced he was the new Russian-speaking censor. And a great disappointment he was too. He was uncooperative, unsociable and flatly refused to take any calls in English, saying he was engaged to censor calls in Russian only and that was exactly what he intended to do. Not even the Colonel's demands or Bill's pleading moved him. There he sat in the corner, in silence, reading his newspaper and sometimes he never turned up at all. But as Mr Molotov didn't seem to want to talk to Mr Maisky, it didn't matter much.

A few weeks after his arrival, I was paired with him for a 4pm duty shift and again Mr X didn't report for work. Bill stayed on to help out but as the only shorthand writer I had to take all the calls that came through in a steady stream. I eventually finished my transcriptions around midnight, arriving home at about 1am to find my mother, as usual, sitting up in bed waiting for me. I sank down to the foot of her bed. 'I am exhausted,' I said. 'And that wretched Mr X never turned up again and didn't even bother to phone to say he wasn't coming.'

Now my mother was doing jury service at the Petty Sessions at the Elephant and Castle in the East End of London on this particular week and she was full of racy stories about the petty criminal underworld, which she would recount with great relish.

'What did you say his name was, dear?' enquired my mother. I repeated it.

'Oh,' said my mother brightly, 'you won't be seeing him for a while, I sent him to prison today.'

'You have done what?' I hissed at her with horror.

'I sent him to prison for three months dear – for receiving stolen goods, office equipment it was ... he said he worked for the Postal and Telegraph Censorship.'

I could scarcely believe my ears ... Whatever happened to all that top-security vetting, what would be the effect on those delicate Anglo-Russian relations, and most important of all, whatever would Mr Churchill say? It was too awful to contemplate.

I didn't bother to undress that night; I scuttled back to the office on the first Underground train. First I phoned Bill who lived in Hadley Green to come in immediately and then, plucking up courage, I phoned the Colonel who didn't seem to be overjoyed to hear my voice at 6.30am.

My mother had her facts absolutely right, and that was the end of Mr X's career in the Radio Department. I never dared ask the Colonel how he explained the whole ghastly incident to the Censorship Sub-Committee and Mr Churchill's reactions can only be imagined.

No new fluent Russian-speaking censor ever reported for duty, and apart from the odd baleful glare from the Colonel, the matter was never referred to again.

As far as I know, Mr Molotov never did want to speak to Mr Maisky and the line to Moscow did not become operational throughout the War.

Through the Canadian National Archive I learnt that they too had a link operating from 1943 from Ottawa to Moscow, but that too was never activated. I have been unable to ascertain whether the service from Washington to Moscow was ever used.

# 8

# THE GERMANS

'The Germans are listening,' the Colonel constantly reminded his staff, expecting them to listen with extra attention, never relaxing their vigilance, however innocent the contents of a call might seem. And we did take the warning seriously, but it was very difficult day after day, month after month and year after year to envisage an ever-alert eavesdropper if you have absolutely no idea of his whereabouts or even of his very existence.

'Are the Germans really listening?' I used to ask Bill, probably after a heavy session with the Ministry of War Transport. 'So they say,' said Bill, who I don't think knew either. Rumour had it that the Germans were stationed on a small boat moored off Hamburg where, it was said, conditions were ideal for intercepting the calls.

I tried the Colonel. 'Do the Germans really listen in to these calls?' The Colonel stared pointedly over my shoulder into space. So I had to accept the fact that I was battling it out with an intangible opponent floating somewhere out there in the ether.

But the Germans were listening to our calls, and very attentively indeed.

In 1941, the *Deutschen Reichpost*, the German equivalent of our GPO, realised that the only telephone link between England and America was the radio circuit using the A3 Scrambler system, and correctly assessed the potential importance of such a link. Their Postal Minister, Wilhelm Ohnesorge, charged a young engineer, Kurt E. Vetterlein, to break the A3's secret parameters and a unit in the Ringstrasse in Berlin was set up to comply with his instruction. The unit was named 'Forschungsantalt' (Research Bureau), and as our own Wireless Telegraphy Board had warned, within a few months, they had cracked the secrets of the A3 system.

By autumn 1941, the unit was already intercepting and descrambling calls from a site that Vetterlein considered to be ideally situated in the coastal resort of Noordwijik in the Netherlands. Equipment filled two rooms of what was previously a youth hostel, and half a dozen highly-qualified interpreters listened in to our transatlantic calls, selecting particular points of Intelligence to translate into English, their elaborate equipment instantly descrambling the conversations.

The Postal Minister was not just a junior minister in the Nazi hierarchy. He was an older man holding Nazi Party Card No. 43, a friend of Hitler and Himmler and SS General Gottlob Berger, and considered his unit's technical feat of breaking through the A3 Scrambler a triumph for German Intelligence. He wrote accordingly to Hitler:

THE REICHPOST MINISTER. Berlin w 66, 6 March 1942.
LEIPSIGER STR. 15

U 5342–1/1 Bfb Nr. 23 gRs.
DECIPHERMENT OF U.S.A. – England Telephone Connection.
SECRET REICH MATTER.

Mein Führer!

The Forschungsanstalt of the Deutchen Reichpost has completed as the latest of its enterprises an intercept installation for
the telephone traffic between the U.S.A. and England, which
has been made unintelligible using all present knowledge of
communications technology. Thanks to the devoted work of
its scientists, it (the D.P.R.) is the only place in Germany that
has succeeded in making the scramble, which had been made
unintelligible with the best methods, again understandable at
the instant of its reception.

I will give the results of our interception to the Reich Leader
of the S.S. Party Comrade Himmler, who will submit them on
March 22.

I will limit the circulation of this communication pending
higher decision in view of the fact that if this success were
to come to the knowledge of the English, they would further
complicate the problem of telephone traffic and cause it to be
sent on by telegraph cable.

Heil mein Führer!
[signed] OHNESORGE.

TO THE:–

Leader and Reich Chancellor
Of the Greater German Reich.
Berlin W8.

To prove the point, the Postal Minister enclosed an example of an intercepted conversation dated 7 September 1941, between two colleagues, the man in America asking for an assistant for a propaganda bureau.

It goes without saying that the Germans were proud and delighted at their spectacular breakthrough, Wilhelm Ohnesorge arranging that intercepts of outstanding interest and Intelligence should be sent immediately to Hitler, who couldn't believe his good fortune that he would be privy to those highly confidential conversations between Churchill and Roosevelt.

Until 1943, the Forschungsanstalt operated more or less without incident; once the AT&T changed the sub-band widths making Vetterlein rethink the enciphering patterns, but translations of all the Churchill/Roosevelt talks landed on the Führer's desk within hours of the calls being made, the unit easily recognising Churchill's voice despite his use of the name 'John Martin'. Nobody was safe from their monitors; they listened to Harry Hopkins, Anthony Eden, Lord Halifax, Averell Harriman, and though an aide to Himmler tried to exaggerate the importance of the material, nothing of great importance was noted until July 1943. The story behind that intercept belongs to another chapter.

Here is an example of a Churchill/Roosevelt call as intercepted by the unit in October 1943. 'A' is identified as the American speaker, 'B' is 'John Martin'.

B. 'John here.'

'Yes.'

'Can you give me any hopeful answer?'

'Yes.'

'Good.'

Churchill then said something 'could be free, open and ...'. Hopkins replied, 'Yes,' which Churchill had to have repeated several times. Then:

A. 'The report (or note) has not yet gone but it will be sent.'

B. 'I see, good.'

'Is that all right?'

'Yes.'

'All right, Goodbye.'

'Goodbye.'

This could have referred to any subject, and I cannot believe that, however enthusiastic the unit was to demonstrate its vigilance, it could have gleaned much information from such an innocuous chat.

Earlier in 1943, our Forces mounted commando raids on the Dutch coast destroying radar systems, and the Forschungsanstalt (now commonly known as 'the Bunker') thought these Allied attacks were getting a little too close for comfort and might endanger their security. The unit was moved to the comparative safety of Valkenswaard, a small town in the southeast of Holland, where their signals could not be detected from the air, for this was too valuable an asset for German Intelligence to lose. To emphasise its high security rating, a twenty-four-hour German Unit from the SS-Pak-Fusiliers mounted guard.

Valkenswaard fitted their needs perfectly. It was only 5 miles from the Belgium border and just south of Eindhoven (home of Phillips & Daf). The field belonging to a local farmer was commandeered by the Germans who started to build their extensive monitoring HQ, forbidding the farmer and all the locals to enter the area. Though called the Bunker, to a casual observer (if any were allowed near the place) it looked anything but. It was specially built to look like a typical Dutch farmhouse, with its technology placed in the underground concrete bunker. Radio masts were discreetly placed in the woods, blending in nicely with its surrounding. There the staff – all thirty-five of them fluent English speakers – lived in luxury where food was specially prepared for them in the kitchen, a living room complete with fireplace and comfortable bedrooms. And apparently, the quality of the reception was good too.

Valkenswaard was the first town in Holland to be liberated by the British Army. A battalion of the Irish Guards under Major Anthony Bailey, after chasing the enemy through Belgium, found the large building conveniently empty for his tired and hungry men. He had no idea it had been used as an important Intelligence unit, for all the technical equipment had vanished.

However, this idyllic existence did not last for too long. Anxious to protect this precious source of Intelligence after the invasion of the European mainland, the unit was on the move again. This time the destination was to be Bavaria. Thankfully the distance from the transmitter considerably impaired the quality of speech and the importance and influence of the Forschungsanstalt Unit obviously waned. Most of the calls intercepted after 1942 were as uninformative as the Churchill call quoted above when our security guidelines were adopted.

Of course, there were lapses in our attention and I suppose a general picture of information was acquired, but apart from one spectacular incident, the unit had to admit that, despite ending the War with huge piles of intercepts, by and large, they provided a disappointing source for high-level Intelligence.

# 9

# A SECURITY CATASTROPHE

In 1943, word came down from 'above' that when a situation arose that necessitated an immediate response or decision on an issue of vital importance, and when there was insufficient time to signal our allies asking their opinion or confirming a joint policy, censorship regulations should be waived and the calls allowed through without interference from the censors. We should be told when the occasion rose. We should take notes but no action. Official thinking foresaw circumstances when a calculated risk was judged to be permissible taking the chance of the enemy overhearing the conversation, but even if they did assess its importance correctly, they would be unable to use the information because the time factor would limit their action.

Such an event arose on 28 July 1943. It is of interest to recall the circumstances that led to the decision to place top-secret information over an open line and the far-reaching effect this had on our future military operations.

In the middle of July, troops under General Eisenhower's command – consisting of British, American and Canadian divisions – invaded Sicily. It was a particularly large combined force but the Allies, realising the chaos on the Italian mainland, hoped for a quick military success. The Germans, also realising the disaffection amongst their partner's morale, tried to stiffen the Italian resistance by reinforcing them with their own troops, but somewhat to the Allies' surprise, their invasion of the island was met with surprisingly little military resistance. Instead of reacting to this situation and adjusting their plans, our High Command failed to recognise the true position, allowing tens of thousands of Axis troops to escape capture.

After the fall of Mussolini, it was well nigh impossible for the Allied High Command to obtain an accurate picture of the situation in mainland Italy. Neither could the War Cabinet judge the intentions of the newly formed Bagdolio Government, suspecting quite rightly that Germany would bring considerable pressure on their partners to continue the War. Another factor to take into consideration was the return to power of King Emmanuel, and this diffused situation was recognised by the War Cabinet. Intelligence had reported that Italy might sue for an Armistice; that we had to treat and negotiate such an agreement was agreed, but before any official talks took place, we needed certain guarantees.

An important factor in our thinking was Churchill's wish to emphasise to the Americans that our sphere of influence lay in the Mediterranean area while President Roosevelt's peace aims had a different emphasis in wanting a total and unconditional surrender of all troops and the Italian government before an Armistice could be discussed. The two leaders sent signals and telegrams continuously to each other but events moved so quickly, making it doubly difficult to reach a policy agreeable to them both.

Churchill wanted the Bagdolio Government to sue us for peace because there was a certain factor that deeply concerned him, and he desperately needed to play for time for a couple of days. This was the fate of our prisoners of war held by the Italians. The Prime Minister remembered all too well the fall of France, when thousands of our men serving there were handed over to the Germans by the French and he was determined that history should not repeat itself in Italy. He wanted to gain a pledge from Bagdolio that our men would remain under his protection until they could be handed over to our military authorities.

The President had now changed his view, agreeing with Churchill's Armistice proposals, but it was imperative the President be given the opportunity to confirm, to wait a couple of days before talks should begin, allowing time for our negotiations for the safety of our men.

On 28 July, the Defence Committee of the War Cabinet met and discussed the dilemma; the need for both leaders to reach a mutual agreement immediately was vital. Finally Churchill was authorised to make a transatlantic call to Roosevelt, asking him to delay his approach to Bagdolio.

I am absolutely sure this decision could not have been taken without considerable debate. After all the Defence Committee knew the score; most of them had used the service regularly, were aware of its sensitivity, and from its inception had regularly warned other users of the need for care and discretion, but the importance of quickly reaching a joint decision

outweighed adoption of the usual, far slower method of signalling and so they took 'that calculated risk'.

This is a transcript of that call made at 1am on 29 July 1943
between Churchill and President Roosevelt:

> CHURCHILL: We do not want proposals for an armistice to
> be made before we have been definitely approached.
> ROOSEVELT: That is correct.
> CHURCHILL: We might as well wait for one or two days.
> ROOSEVELT: That is right.

Then there is talk about the British prisoners of war in Italy
whose transportation to 'the land of the Hun' should be
avoided. Churchill would, therefore, contact the King of Italy,
and Roosevelt said he too would contact Emmanuel.

'I do not quite know how I shall do that,' said the President.

Churchill has been criticised – unfairly in my opinion – for
'leaking like a sieve', but he too was well aware of the risks
of speaking frankly for what was less than a couple of minutes' conversation prompted by his concern for our prisoners
of war. He had used the service so many times as a matter
of routine, day and night, a call at one in the morning was
nothing unusual; neither was his somewhat dramatic use of
language. Churchill used language – even in ordinary day conversation – in a special style mixing somewhat extravagant
sentiments with normal everyday speech. However late the
hour, and however well he had dined, I can say that this factor
never impaired his judgement of what was proper to mention,
and I considered him no more a security risk than, say, Harry
Hopkins or Roosevelt.

The Germans intercepted the call from their special unit
situated on the Dutch coast at Noordwijk, interpreted its

meaning correctly, and acted immediately on the analysis of their Intelligence. Within hours, the translation of the contents of the call, including the identities of the speakers, had landed on Hitler's desk. Within two days, they had redeployed their troops to reinforce those divisions surviving the Sicilian campaign and rushed further divisions from the north to the south of Italy.

Unfortunately, the Allies encountered further delays to their plans to invade the Italian mainland, and it seems too that General Eisenhower and the Allied High Command were unaware of the heavy build-up of German troops. When we invaded Salerno on 9 September, our forces met unexpectedly heavy opposition.

Never again was top-secret military information placed over the Radio line. Never again was such sensitive material allowed through on the 'calculated risk' theory, and though the Department was aware of the ruling, we were never told the reasons behind such a decision.

Vetterlein's work and the hopes of the Forschungsanstalt had been fully justified, and the Germans considered this incident to be one of their finest Intelligence coups of the War.

# 10

# 'SIGSALY'

It was now obvious to everybody on both sides of the Atlantic that the Transatlantic Radio line was an imperfect tool to handle such high-security traffic, even with its rules and regulations. Lacking a truly safe communication link across the Atlantic was now more than just a nuisance, it had become a top-level priority to find a more advanced type of scrambler that could be used to ensure complete protection for a two-way conversation, and one which could not be intercepted and its signals broken down by a third party.

For many years, in fact long before the War commenced, American communication, signals experts and scientists had been experimenting with various forms of voice-coding and voice-decoding machines. The Bell Telephone Company of New York had begun work as early as 1920 on various voice privacy schemes, but with the advent of war, experiment and sheer hard graft by their engineering teams had moved scientific advances to a point where experimental prototypes were being assembled in their New York laboratories.

In the beginning, it was known as the 'X System' only to those who worked on it. To the team in the American Signal Corps working alongside the Bell Telephone engineers, it became known as 'the X-Ray System' or 'Sigsaly'. That remains its public title to this day.

The project was important historically (apart from its role during the War) as the pioneering digital speech transmission system employing a form of pulse code modulation and it was one of the starting points of the digital transmission age that followed.

The Americans were naturally proud of their breakthrough in this particular field of speech protection, and it is understandable to a certain extent that they wished to keep the principles of their scientific work under a blanket of high security. As early as 1940, Mr W.G.I. Radley from the GPO had written asking The Bell Telephone Company for design information, hinting that it was to be used for a secrecy system for ourselves, and though The Bell Telephone Company obliged by sending some information, it apparently stimulated the American team to perfect work just that bit harder in order to be the first in the field.

It seems they were extremely complicated machines to build because they consisted of such a large number of parts. Many were unpatented at that time (and some remained so as late as 1975). Nevertheless, after extensive tests over many months, three terminals were said to be ready for installation in 1943, one in London, one in Washington and one in North Africa.

Bill had a friend in 'high places' who used to pass on to us the latest gossip and rumours (it was no good relying on the Colonel to tell us anything), and our informant heard it whispered that the Americans had invented a wonder machine that would put us censors out of work.

The story of 'Sigsaly' unfolded slowly over the months like instalments in a spy thriller – sometimes just within the realm of credibility and sometimes, it must be admitted, quite hilariously.

In February 1943, General Ismay minuted the Prime Minister about the arrival in London of an American officer, Major Miller of the War Department, who wished to discuss the system of speech secrecy equipment to be used for Transatlantic Radio calls. Major Miller had made several important demands that, from the tone of General Ismay's Minute, rather surprised the War Cabinet and CIGS.

Apparently the machine was enormous, needing three empty rooms to house it and six men to operate it. In fact, it weighed in at 18 tons and was shipped over on the *Queen Elizabeth* on 15 July 1943. Major Miller also insisted that American Army Signal personnel should be in sole charge of its operation and guarded exclusively by them, the inference being that the Americans did not wish our experts to become too familiar with its technique.

The Chiefs of Staff had considered the position and thought it essential to establish beyond doubt the effectiveness of the equipment. They proposed sending Dr Alan Turing, director of the Government Code and Cipher School at Bletchley Park, to New York to obtain his opinion on the 'X-Ray System', for if it was not 100 per cent secure, it would be extremely dangerous to use. General Ismay commented to the Prime Minister that he thought the American desire to retain complete control of the apparatus was strange, but felt the time would come when it was installed and its value proved, and so asked to be let into its secrets.

Later in February, Dr Turing sent in his report saying, with certain qualifications, that in his opinion, the machine would be adequate. He also commented that if the equipment was to be operated only by Americans, there was nothing to stop them listening in to British conversations if they so wished. Mr Beer of the GPO had also been to the Bell Laboratory in New York, but had not been given the full facilities for examination that had been accorded to Dr Turing as they would not permit him to include certain details and drawings in his report.

A month later General Sir Hastings Ismay updated the Prime Minister, outlining the latest American proposals for using their new speech secrecy equipment. They insisted that the main set should be installed at their Communications Centre, and until extensions were ready for use in the War Cabinet Rooms in Great George Street, all users would be required to make transatlantic calls from there. Anyway, President Roosevelt wanted nothing to do with the scheme, but gave no reason. And where was the American Communication Centre situated? In Selfridges' Annex basement.

There is always, or so it seems to me, an element of farce attending high-level, top-secret security equipment; 'cloak and dagger' attitudes of secrecy appear to enter the souls of otherwise sane and sensible men and outrageous suggestions are put forward on an agenda without a thought of how in practice they could possibly be implemented.

Another minute to the War Cabinet and Chiefs of Staff gave more details of these ground rules set out by ETOUSA (European Theatre of Operations, USA). Only a very restricted list of speakers confined to top brass at the War Office, Admiralty, Air Ministry and Combined Operations Headquarters, Churchill and Anthony Eden were permitted to make a call – no civilian member of the War Cabinet or ministries were authorised. The service was only operational between 1400 and 2000 hours, calls had to be pre-booked by ringing the embassy at least an hour beforehand, giving names of speakers involved on both sides of the Atlantic, and on arrival at the Communication Centre (Selfridges' Annex), must show their special identification passes.

It really does not need a great deal of imagination to gauge Churchill's reactions to these extraordinary schemes. Did the Americans have no idea at all of the Prime Minister's daily routine, the regular eighteen-hour day worked by his staff, or come to that, of their own War Administration who regularly used the phone at night? The Bell Telephone Company must have thought a war is like a commercial business, keeping to a strict office timetable and restricting telephone calls to a few favoured members of the staff.

Things were not proceeding that smoothly on the other side of the Atlantic either. By October 1943, the extension to the White House had yet to be installed and had only got as far as the Public Health building about 3 miles away. No wonder the President wanted nothing to do with it.

Dr Turing's warning to the War Cabinet that the Americans could, while retaining sole management of the system, listen in to British calls, was duly taken to heart, and this is where I come into the story. As our interests were involved, it was proposed that we appoint a stenographer to listen and record conversations but with no authority to disrupt them.

I was approached 'unofficially' and not through the Department, and was asked if I would care to work in the American Communications HQ, in Selfridges' Department Store working regular hours and, for the icing on the cake, it might be possible to get me onto the American payroll where I would pay no income tax on my greatly increased salary. It sounded like heaven – on the No. 13 bus route, next to Selfridges' Food Department where I would immediately register for food rations. No indecision, no thinking it over, I said, 'Yes please'.

All too good to be true, and, of course, I never heard another word.

Obviously, with such complicated and pioneering equipment, it took months of tests, overcoming various technical difficulties, before all the snags could be ironed out. Even in October 1943, of four test calls made, all were ineffective. It was not until April 1944, that 'Sigsaly' became truly operational.

But the truth to tell, Churchill did not use this telephone very often to speak to the President – and I suspect, for a number of reasons.

Robert Price is an American expert on ciphers and communication systems and has researched extensively into the use of 'Sigsaly'. His theory is that shortly after 'Sigsaly' started working, Churchill booked a call to the President who, upon hearing Churchill's voice, started laughing. Later, Churchill, wondering why, made enquiries and was told that the equipment distorted his voice and the President thought he sounded like Donald Duck. Churchill apparently remarked that 'he would never use that damn thing again'.

That sort of jokey remark would never have been resented by Churchill; one could name many faults in his character, but he was never petty or touchy and this was certainly not sufficient reason for his only occasional use of 'Sigsaly'.

Professor Warren Kimball's compilation and comment in *Churchill and Roosevelt, The Complete Correspondence* comes nearer to an exact explanation, that too frequent contact could trivialise their relationship, and the President was not a 'telephone man', fearing he may be pressed into decisions he would later regret.

My theory is much simpler. I feel sure that Churchill, the War Cabinet and the CIGS, were irritated by American insistence that the equipment could only be handled by American personnel and their refusal to discuss the technical principles of the system. After all, the Allies had agreed to pool scientific knowledge, but I imagine that the Bell Telephone Company – with an eye to years to come – knew they had achieved a real winner with enormous commercial possibilities with the invention of their digital transmission system and wished to protect their research. The prototype machines were extremely expensive to build, costing a reputed million dollars each and in fact, only twelve of them were completed.

Maybe that too explains the excessive exclusiveness of the names allowed to use 'Sigsaly' for even the Deputy Prime Minister, Clement Attlee, was absent from the official list. But most of all, it was so inconvenient. There were no extensions to the War Office, Admiralty, Air Ministry or Foreign Office and most important of all, to Churchill's flat in Downing Street where he usually worked either at his desk or in bed. Using 'Sigsaly' meant going down to the War Cabinet Rooms between 2pm and 8pm – not times of the day particularly suited to his working routine – and so he did not avail himself of the service too often. Perhaps the 'opening hours' were deliberately framed to discourage a certain speaker from making late-night phone calls. By the summer of 1943, those dark and desperate days of 1942 had passed when personal contact between Churchill and Roosevelt was so essential, and the bonds of friendship were cemented. Now they had regular meetings at conferences, their respective staffs had good lines of communication going and the need for frequent calls had ended.

Much more acceptable was the service offered by the Radio Department – functioning twenty-four hours a day, within its known limitations and, providing speakers behaved with propriety, was used up to capacity to handle the transatlantic traffic. Certainly we lost some of the high-ranking American Embassy/Washington traffic, though the routine stuff was still handled by us and I can truthfully say – even from this distance in time – that 'Sigsaly' made little difference to our workload.

'Sigsaly' did earn its own unique place in history during its brief existence, quite apart from its pioneering technical principles. Down the years, from as early as the 1920s, many gifted electronic engineers had worked on the project, including a most unlikely contributor – Hedy Lamarr, the film star. Her first husband, an Austrian, was an engineer and from him she had picked up a certain amount of knowledge. With an engineering partner she had perfected one of the machine's parts and had it patented under her name.

President Roosevelt died on 12 April 1945, and our Radio Department wondered if any calls to Washington would come through us. First it was rumoured that the King wished to speak to Mrs Roosevelt, but to my knowledge, no member of the Royal Family ever called the States. We knew that Churchill had never spoken to Harry Truman, and that first historic call to the new President was made on 'Sigsaly'. Thence after, he was cabling and signalling daily to Truman in the manner used for Roosevelt.

On 25 April, Churchill learnt that Himmler, friend and confidante of Hitler and instigator of some of Germany's most murderous policies, had approached the Allies making private peace overtures, and wished to open peace negotiations ignoring Hitler. Immediately, Churchill spoke to Truman and broke all the records, making the longest call ever, a two-hour discussion on how the Allies should react and coordinate their policies as to what was now obvious – the collapse of Nazi Germany.

After the War, all twelve 'Sigsaly' machines were dismantled. Its monument is the fascination of its technical originality, and it is still a subject for writing and discussion by cryptologists the world over.

But it is not entirely accurate for the Americans and Germans to claim that as soon as 'Sigsaly' became operational, the Radio Department handled only calls from minor civil servants and the middle echelon of officialdom. I would have hardly thought that members of the War Cabinet, the ministers in charge of the all-important supply ministries qualified under that heading. Moreover, I do not believe that our Washington Embassy, our Joint Staff Mission and other agencies operating in Washington were favoured with an extension, though I have no means of confirming this theory. Our very busy line to Ottawa was not part of the 'Sigsaly' system and by the latter part of 1943, new categories of callers were authorised to use the service, adding to our workload.

The governments in exile in London, the French, Dutch, Norwegians and especially the Poles all had bureaux and representatives in Washington and were in constant touch with each other. The Polish head of the London government, Mr Mikolajczyk, used the line frequently, for discussions had begun between Churchill, Eden and Stalin on the future boundaries of Poland. All the representatives of the occupied countries, but especially Poland, were acutely conscious that their political future needed to be carefully protected if they were to inherit and return to their homeland when the Germans had been defeated. These political and military heads of governments were all possessors of high-level, top-secret information and so were subject to the same level of attention accorded to all users of the service. It is a romantic notion to believe that Churchill and Roosevelt were the only guardians of vital secrets.

## 11

# A VISIT TO AN RAF AIRFIELD & CHANGES IN DEPARTMENT POLICY

On the evening of 16 May 1943, the Colonel summoned me. 'Get the early morning train to Lincoln where you will be met at the station by an RAF driver. I understand you know how to deal with this sort of situation.' No more explanations were forthcoming, he merely handed me a rail pass.

I was delighted to escape out of Union House into the country. It was nearly eighteen months since I had been sent on a travelling job and I thought my present work had superseded any previous experience and my name erased from the rotas.

The usually packed train took hours to reach Lincoln, it stopped at every station, village and hamlet but the spring countryside looked green and fresh and it was wonderful to be away from the devastation and dereliction of the city.

Lincoln station was teeming with RAF and after a process of elimination, I found my driver, introduced myself by showing my Departmental pass, and off we drove through the flat Lincolnshire countryside to the aerodrome (I guessed that was to be my destination). I had previously only been on Fighter

Command stations, and this was my first posting to a Bomber Station. It had an unfinished look to it; buildings were scattered, the hangars were enormous, maintenance sheds and personnel quarters were sited away from the main drome. So I wasn't exactly surprised when we sped by the buildings, though I was quite unprepared for my new quarters – a Nissen hut on what looked to me like the edge of the airfield. I remember getting out of the car, the wind gusting across the flat countryside, wondering why I had been delivered to such a remote site, even in the name of 'top security'. A young Flying Officer greeted me with no great enthusiasm.

'We had no idea they would send a girl, I thought a censor would be a man.'

'But what difference does it make?' I said, and proceeded to tell him of my varied and considerable experience of censorship matters. I had come to realise that public perception of a censor was male, middle-aged, humourless and totally lacking the milk of human kindness.

'But we were not expecting a girl. The fact is,' and he turned a delicate shade of pink, 'there are no – er – washroom facilities here and the main WAAF quarters are closed and you are to be on continual duty for twenty-four hours.'

I looked out of the window. About 25yds away were some scrubby bushes. Oh well – for King and Country – it could be far worse.

That out of the way, we got down to business. There was to be a complete and total security blackout of the station. The post boxes had already been sealed; no personnel had either been allowed in or out of the camp for some days and the entire telephone switchboard was to close down. All had been warned that if any calls to the outside world were made and detected (by me), they would be put on a charge.

The bank of terminals was larger than I had ever worked before. Not only were the usual NAAFI and Mess lines hooked up, but every phone in the Adjutant's Office, the WAAF quarters, Ordinance, and Maintenance offices as well. I believe only the Station Commander had an outside line.

With all these security precautions being set in motion, it was now obvious that something big was afoot. Bombing raids deep into Germany including Berlin had been nightly occurrences for some time, but, I wondered, what warranted all these extra precautions?

With memories of the Norwegian debacle, I sent off the Flight Officer to the main switchboard and we checked carefully every line. By now the blackout was in force – at about 4pm. There was no sign of any life on the airfield, the station seemed deserted and lifeless and I was not at all sure whether I would like spending the night alone in my remote fastness. After a couple of hours of nothing, a much older Warrant Officer arrived announcing he would be on duty with me throughout the night. Very good company he was too, regaling me with stories of when he joined the Royal Flying Corps in the First World War, the Sopwith Pups and other ramshackle planes he had flown, adventures and tall stories galore. Not a word about our present situation, no questions were asked, neither of us would embarrass the other.

He had influence too with the NAAFI because then all sorts of meals and refreshments started to be delivered and kept on coming through the night. I was beginning to relax and enjoy myself … until …

Around dusk, all hell broke loose. I had never heard such a dreadful, deafening din in all my life. I had, after all, lived through the London Blitz, survived bombs coming down within 100yds, listened to Ack Ack fire, but never anything like this. Our hut shook, rattled and rocked, I was taking no chances, for I was sure we were being dive-bombed by enemy planes and promptly hid under the desk, till my highly amused companion bawled above the noise, 'Come on – they're our planes taking off.'

My guess was correct in believing our hut was situated on the edge of the airfield; what I didn't reckon with was that it would be on the end of the runway. Huge Lancaster bombers – I could see their loaded bomb bays – flew, so it seemed to me, just a few feet above our roof. One after another with only a few minutes' interval between them, taking off, flying into the approaching night sky. Once one's ears got accustomed to the noise, I could appreciate the drama of the moment, wonder about their target for the night, and wish them all Godspeed and a safe return.

We returned to watch our switch panel. It had been so fitted that a flickering light would indicate if a telephone call was being made, but not once had we seen it. So far, so good. But a twenty-four-hour watch had been ordered, which I had every intention of carrying out. I worried too about the raid; reading about nightly RAF raids, the mounting losses of men and machines were part of the price of war and however much one sympathised with their families, reading daily reports about our bombing raids had, because of their regularity, become a routine feature of wartime life. Now it was different. I was only remotely connected with the raid, would never meet any of the men taking part, yet from now on I would understand the suspense, the waiting for the returning aircraft, the relief on hearing the throb of their engines.

It was a very long night. Just as the sky was beginning to lighten, the sound of aircraft and the roar of their engines filled the hut and we rushed outside to watch the planes land. But how different they looked from a few hours earlier. My first and lasting impression was how dirty their fuselage had become – from the flak I supposed – and how battered and damaged the few that landed looked. We waited hopefully for more planes to come in and my companion thought some of the aircraft might well have landed at other stations. I hoped fervently that he was right.

All through the long night's watch, not once did that reliable light flicker on our panel, and I gave the station full marks for discipline and security mindedness.

At about lunchtime, the Flying Officer arrived to tell me the watch was over, he had fixed up with a kind soul in the village to let me have a bath and a rest in her home and my driver would later take me to Lincoln to catch the evening train back home.

I thanked them both for their consideration and their care for my well-being, especially as far more pressing matters must have occupied their thoughts. As I stepped into the car I remember asking quite casually the name of the station: 'Scampton – and good wishes from 617 Squadron,' was the answer.

I learnt – along with the rest of the country – of the destination of 617 Squadron on that now-famous raid, their target, and the success of that daring but costly operation on the Moehne and Eder Dams. I was highly amused at the reference in Paul Brinkhill's book *The Dambusters*, when he described the abortive efforts of the Scampton switchboard trying to ring Lord Portal, then dining with Roosevelt in Washington, to tell him of their success in breaching the Dams. They should have consulted the expert out in the sticks. Work at Union House seemed rather mundane after that trip, though there was no letting up on the number of calls we handled.

Some time towards the end of 1943, I developed frozen shoulder, tennis elbow and writer's cramp all at the same time. The doctor prescribed a period of less intensive writing, so I asked the Colonel if the Department could run to a typewriter – at least, I thought, I could type out my transcriptions.

'No,' said the Colonel, 'You might make a copy and take it out of the Department.' I was furious and thought he was taking the matter of security to absurd lengths and said so. He never relented over the typewriter issue but sent me off to HQ, for forthcoming military operations were to be discussed. These proved to be of little interest to our Radio Department, being mostly discussions on internal censorship and security during the coming months.

Back home again, the lines positively buzzed during late 1943 and the first months of 1944. The Germans noted the increased activity too but complained they got little specific information from this source. The Supply Ministries worked everything out using their usual procedures of pre-signalling, then phoning through comment and confirmation of arrangements and there was a lot of to-ing and fro-ing of ministers and a general air of expectation was abroad.

After the excitement of the invasion, almost imperceptibly, the nature and content of the calls changed. From previously being the most convenient channel available for both us and the Americans to arrange meetings and discuss supply problems, another category of speaker seemed to have received sponsorship. These calls had political and humanitarian overtones, and I found them particularly worrying to deal with, as they fell into a grey area not covered by our precise rules. The ordering of relief supplies was fairly straightforward; it was the discussion of forward-looking plans and policy that bothered me. Charles Monnet was an old customer of ours who was closely connected with General de Gaulle and the Free French Forces but also worked with the British Purchasing Mission in Washington. Now he started speaking to a new name, Maurice Schumann, and they were discussing ideas such as the early rehabilitation of industrial output when Europe was finally liberated. In fact, they were exploratory talks on the eventual setting up of The Iron, Coal and Steel Community.

If it was obvious to me, then it must be to the Germans, that these were plans for the dismemberment of industrial Germany. Though Monsieur Monnet assured me he was empowered to discuss these matters over the line, I asked Bill to get us, through the Colonel, if not in detail then some sort of guideline whereby we could judge whether it was desirable for the enemy to learn of our future plans for Germany after their defeat. Of course, I should have known better. Back came the message, 'Use your common sense and judgement'. I made absolutely sure that these conversations were permissible over an 'open line' and was eventually told that 'the highest authority had agreed'. That was alright then.

I must confess now that Monsieur Monnet was my particular star of all the exiled governments living and working in London. Most of them were worried almost to death about the fate of their country and their loved ones. The Poles, Norwegians, the Danish, Dutch and French had bureaux in London and all of them made use of the TRL extensively and circumstances did not make for cheerful listening. But Monsieur Monnet was different. Brimming with Gaelic charm and a delightful French accent, along with Monsieur Schumann, they were energetic and positive about their plans for rebuilding Europe. I had seen news in the cinema of the appalling devastation across Europe and applauded their enthusiasm and plans. From then on, all through my life, I have watched with interest (and sometimes dismay) at the European Institutions and their policies. When I was about seventy-five I did a Birnbeck College Course of post-war European history. I visited the European Parliament in Strasbourg, the European Court of Justice in Luxembourg and the Commission in Brussels and paid my respects to Monsieur Schumann's house where he was born in Luxembourg, painted a bright European blue.

So I was particularly thrilled when Lord Patten presented the Churchill Museum with the coveted Council of Europe Museum Award 2006. I wonder whether I am the only one alive who listened to those original explanatory talks.

Another group of speakers worried me too. The Relief Agencies started making far-reaching plans to follow our victorious armies to ameliorate the suffering and deprivation suffered by the local population. I remember being particularly concerned about Sir Frederick Leith Ross, the Head of UNRRA (United Nations Rehabilitation and Relief Association), speaking regularly to American colleagues and the BPM. His first theatre of operation was in Greece, a particularly sensitive area where Germany would welcome information in 1944. Again no official advice except, 'It won't hurt the Germans to know how confident we are of total victory.'

By now, I had become thoroughly irritated by the lack of advice and direction from above and there seemed nobody to ask except Bill and he wasn't in the Colonel's confidence either. Neither of us wanted to go over the Colonel's head and appeal to higher authority – even if we knew who that was.

And something else nagged at the back of my mind, which Bill and I discussed quietly alone. If, as we were constantly reminded, the Germans monitored all the calls, was some of the subject matter contained in them deliberately misleading?

The word 'misinformation' was unheard of then – but our open line seemed to us the ideal method for 'planting' information. But how would I ever know if this happened? If the Colonel or Bill didn't warn us to let a call through without interference, at the first smell of an indiscretion, the speaker would be cut off. Anyway, our panel of speakers was comparatively small, we should be aware of any artificial change of subject. Surely the Colonel would take us into his confidence.

Only on one occasion in, I think, late 1944 or 1945, did I have cause to wonder. The calls were a mystery then as they are now, and though I have made a few enquiries, I have read nothing during these intervening years that throws any light on the matter.

The Colonel motioned me to the monitoring position and handed me a docket naming two unknown (to me) speakers. For the first time I could remember, he sat down beside me and unhooked the small extra earpiece on my telephone while I put on my headphones. He took only casual interest in the early Churchill/Roosevelt calls and rarely listened to the entire conversation.

The London speaker read out a series of mathematical calculations at top speed. He had a shrill, very distinctive staccato-like delivery, spoke very quickly and I lost the gist early on, but the Colonel made a gesture not to bother with a shorthand record, so I merely listened. The American speaker appeared to be checking the figures. There was no interruption from my American colleague so I assumed she had been told to let it go too. Several calls of this nature went out, then after a few weeks, they stopped as suddenly as they started. Alas, I cannot remember the names of the speakers though I can still hear that distinctive voice in my memory.

I should have been even more alarmed if I had known of the enormous importance the Germans attached to monitoring our service, for I had no inkling then of this extraordinary cat and mouse exercise being played out over the airwaves between the three protagonists. I think if I had known then that translations of the Churchill calls landed within two hours on Hitler's desk, I should have downed pencils and made a run for it.

# 12

# CALLS TO REMEMBER

One week after the invasion of Europe, long before the excitement had died down, and the feeling that at long last, the tides of war were turning in our favour, the first V1 of thousands to be launched against us arrived in the South East bringing with them, at the very least, inconvenience and dislocation to our lives, and tragedy for those unfortunate enough to find themselves directly beneath its flight path.

Along with the many other Londoners, our Hampstead flat was severely damaged, and we too became 'bombed out', so this was our opportunity to move while it had to be extensively repaired. I had asked – and Bill had backed me – that if I worked later than midnight, I could ask for a car and driver from 'the pool' to take me home. The Colonel thought that a rotten idea and wondered why I couldn't use the Underground as usual – it ran till about 2am.

The Underground started to fill up again with shelterers, not in such numbers as during the Blitz, and the atmosphere was different too. In an odd sort of way, we civilians felt a common ground with our men battling it out in Europe, and though thousands of Londoners died during the onslaught, we knew we could manage to hang on till the rocket launch sites at Peenemünde were captured. The nightly wireless description of the devastation and the appalling plight of the civilians in occupied Europe somehow made our troubles appear negligible.

My own particular man had been fighting it out in various countries since 1941. Now he wrote cheerfully from Gracie Fields' villa on the Isle of Capri where he was recovering from an appendix operation, still enquiring how many millions of troops' letters I had read. I was never able to tell him that real life for me in the Censorship started about a fortnight after he left for the Middle East. I knew his movements after El Alamein, when he was posted to Middle East HQ in Cairo, living in some luxury for eighteen months. Thereafter, he kept vanishing for months at a time (I was quite distracted with worry), then turning up again in Bari in Italy, disappearing again and finally surfacing in Salonika, Greece. I wondered what he was up to. His letters to me were cryptic and mysterious, but then so were mine to him. We would certainly have a lot of explaining to do and much to talk about.

Everybody, but everybody in the country had a 'bomb story' to recount, whether they lived in the towns or in the remotest part of the rural countryside. It had become our national conversation topic, so here is a good place to tell mine.

At Finchley Road Underground Railway Line, the train comes out of the tunnel to open but still underground level, so there are long flights of stairs up to the ticket office at street level at West Hampstead Station, where I left the train. At the top of the stairs, I was thrown roughly to the ground by a rugby tackle from a very large man who sprawled on top of me. 'Help! Help!' I whimpered ... this was just too much. The man on top of me said, 'Be quiet, you fool – don't you know there is a doodlebug overhead and the engine has just cut out.' Within seconds, there was an enormous explosion, the waiting room shook and heaved and bits of plaster fell off the ceiling. When the noise abated, the man scrambled off me, pulled me to my feet and said politely, 'Goodnight Miss – have a safe journey home,' and walked off. I set off unsteadily up West End Lane to find my mother wandering about, shouting my name and looking for me. She said, 'This is ridiculous. You must get "that man" to get a driver to bring you home.'

One day I broke the rules and crawled under the barrier at the foot of Union House stairs, went upstairs and found two possible rooms that could be turned into Restrooms for the staff. I wondered if the Colonel plus the Ministry of Works could actually cooperate before the end of the War and find some chairs and a table. I thought it doubtful, but the problem solved itself because we became a victim of the V1s and had to find somewhere to live; 'Anywhere,' I told Ma, 'but it MUST be on the Central Line.' We ended up in a huge attic in a hotel on Bayswater Road.

During my three and a half years in the Department, I must have handled some hundreds of calls, the Radio Unit itself some thousands, even the Germans admitted to listening in to up to sixty calls a day and sending off their transcriptions to their General High Command.

Obviously, memory has blurred the contents of the large majority of calls, only the personalities of the speakers themselves remain undiminished by time. Two separate conversations I remember with startling clarity, and have haunted me down the years. Both took place in the last months of the War; both in their way illustrate very clearly the tragedy of a country and the character of the speaker.

The first call took place, if my memory is accurate, in the first weeks of August 1944. The question of Poland's future borders had always occupied the mind of Churchill and the War Cabinet. Churchill particularly felt a sentimental attachment to Poland and had discussed, argued and fought hard in talks with Stalin over the past years for their borders to bear some resemblance to their original outline. Mr Mikolajczk had exerted considerable pressure on the Allies to further their claims, but though we always demonstrated our continual support for the Polish cause, the sheer impracticability of sending a military force to support the Warsaw uprising in the late summer of 1944 was obvious.

The Russian armies had advanced to within a few miles of Warsaw to the banks of the Vistula River. Despite an emotional plea from Churchill to Stalin, the Russian troops and their High Command made no effort at all to send either troops or arms in support of the Polish Underground Army in their fierce struggle against the Germans. They merely watched the terrible drama being played out a few miles away.

I was alone on night duty and it was certainly after midnight when I received a booking from a Polish Army General in London who wished to speak to an American Air Force General in Washington. Both of their names were on our list of sponsored speakers and there was no reason why I should not sanction their call; within a few minutes I was rung by the Faraday operator informing me that my speakers were ready to commence.

I found my Polish General extremely hard to understand; firstly, his English was poor and heavily accented, and secondly, he appeared to be in a very emotional state and however much I tried to concentrate, I simply could not get the drift of what he was trying to say. Neither did the American General, who was shouting down the line impatiently. Then after a minute, I heard my General say, 'Roosevelt'. The penny dropped, and I couldn't get to the 'Off' switch quickly enough to disconnect the call.

This was the time, I thought, to break the most important Department rule, 'NEVER give the speakers our private telephone number'. But this was obviously an instance when the General had to understand the implications of speaking on an open line and I told him to ring me immediately. He did so and in considerable distress told me of the military tragedy and the dreadful story of the Polish patriots uprising in Warsaw; how they were fighting back with steadily decreasing fire power; how the survivors of the previous Jewish uprising in the ghetto had joined the patriots, but their defence was hopeless if the Allies did not come to their immediate aid. It seems there had been several attempts before to get an air-drop through to Poland by British aircraft based in Italy but their losses had been heavy, so the Chiefs of Staff had decided regretfully that there would be no more flights because they were impractical, Warsaw being beyond their flying range. Now, said the General, this was the last desperate attempt to save his country. He wanted to appeal personally to President Roosevelt to order in his long-distance bombers, the 3.24s to bomb the German positions in and outside Warsaw – only this could save Warsaw and give time to urge the Russians to come to their help.

I explained to him, as gently as I could, that a call of this nature, however desperate the situation, could not go over an open line. The Germans were monitoring our conversation, the German Luftwaffe were by no means a spent force and to let such a request go over the airwaves would undoubtedly endanger the planes and their crew, and in all consciousness, I could not allow it. He should use his usual signalling system to the States. He pleaded that it would take too long and I realised he found it very hard to accept my decision. I used to think, that at this moment, he finally came to terms with reality, that the Poland he knew had gone forever and that he would never return to his homeland.

I spent the rest of the night writing out a full report of the incident, in which I admitted to breaking the rules in speaking personally to the caller, and laid it carefully on the Colonel's desk for immediate attention. He made no comment to me at all.

The last word must belong to Churchill. Every detail of that particular call remains vividly in my memory: the time of day, my own plans and circumstances and the events leading up to it.

The Doodlebug era was over, but the V2 rockets were still a part of our lives, dropping unannounced from the skies, causing widespread havoc and fatalities. Again, there seemed nothing one could do – not even our anti-aircraft fire could catch them so we patiently waited for the launching sites to be put out of action by our Forces.

I was doing a rare early Saturday morning duty from 9am to about 5 in the afternoon and, even rarer, I was having a Sunday off returning to duty on Monday evening. I was expecting a nice quiet shift with just a few routine calls.

At midday, Union House rocked on its foundations. Articles on the desks landed on the floor and the lights swayed on their hangings, and whatever it was, it was far too close for comfort. Within a few minutes ARP Heavy Rescue lorries, the Fire Brigade and a stream of ambulances were rushing down Cheapside. We heard that a V2 had dropped about half a mile down the road near Holborn Circus, onto the crowded market at Leather Lane. As usual, the Saturday morning market was packed – vegetables and fruit were hard to come by and Leather Lane Market always had well-stocked stalls – it was a real favourite with Londoners and we guessed that casualties must have been very heavy indeed. That supposition was confirmed when I walked down Newgate Street at lunchtime and talked to members of the ARP.

At this time, Anthony Eden was on one of his frequent trips to Ottawa. Nevertheless, I was slightly surprised when John Martin booked a call to him during the afternoon. I thought it must be the real John Martin this time, but no – it was the Boss. His usual grunt indicating that he was ready and by which I could now decipher his mood, sounded subdued and serious. Imagine my reactions when after greeting Anthony Eden, Churchill said, 'This morning at twelve o'clock …'. I reached immediately for the 'Off' switch.

'I must remind you Sir that there should be no mention of any damage suffered from enemy aircraft on the line. Would you like your call reconnected?'

An acknowledging grunt.

'Anthony, this morning …'. He sounded so upset, but I had no option other than to disconnect him again and warn him of the dangers of an open line. I sat there waiting for the blast of disapproval that in a more cheerful mood could well follow such temerity on my part, but no – quietly he replaced the receiver. There was no doubt about it, he was grief-stricken over quite one of the worst bombing incidents that had hit London since the Blitz.

Of the two occasions that Churchill flouted the Censorship rules, one was deliberately planned, this other an immediate and emotional response to the plight of ordinary men and women. Compassion was the emotion that prompted this last impulsive action. Nobody could deny that he was the most unpredictable man to work for and so many adjectives detrimental to his character can be levelled at him, but for me, one of his most endearing qualities contributing to his greatness lay in his ability to identify with ordinary people.

There was another quality about that call that makes me remember it so vividly – the stillness in both our rooms. Mine was easily explained, but not in the Prime Minister's room. Usually it was full of background noise when making/taking calls in bed, there would be the rustling of papers, occasional crashes and tinkle of glass with his favourite water/whisky, but now he seemed to be quite alone. Then I looked at the time; it was 4pm in the afternoon – nap time. That was the time when nobody was allowed to disturb his afternoon sleep, this time somebody had. And his first reaction – despite years of discipline – had been to grab that telephone to tell Eden of the tragedy.

I was greatly privileged to have been able to listen to Churchill in conversation over those three and a half years. I realised then, young as I was and inexperienced in assessing character, that compared to other politicians and personalities of that era, only he, with his almost inhuman capacity for work, his exceptional personality, his gift of language and oratory that inspired the nation, could lead us to victory. In my humble estimation, he was truly unique.

# 13

# END OF AN ERA

All eight of us gathered in Union House on 8 May 1945 when the Colonel at last allowed us to lay down our pencils and stop work. The War was over – VE Day had been declared. There was no reason for censorship; after all, surely the Germans must have stopped monitoring the calls too. I took the last call at 10.30 am on VE day. We could scarcely believe we had won, and come through those dreadful years unscathed. No more night work, no more blackout, just a slow transition to peacetime and a future life with our loved ones for us all.

Within its limitations, and there were many, including the use of clumsy equipment and little interest or direction from those who instigated the Department, we wondered if we had been successful in our objectives. Nobody in authority had ever really given us any indication that we were doing an effective job or even of the very existence of the Deutschen Reichpost Unit. Perhaps because we served two masters, the Post Office who maintained the technical aspect of the service and the Postal and Telegraph Censorship authorities within the Ministry of Information who were responsible to the War Cabinet, we were thought capable of making our own responsible decisions and forming sensible security policies.

I had always assumed, during both the actual War and then down the years, that we were subject – however insubstantial my evidence was – to the fact that the Intelligence Agencies knew about the Department, and the meagre information we were given was at their direction. But research has done nothing to prove the theory. In fact, research has provided little evidence of our actual existence at all.

I am assured that my notes of the Churchill/Roosevelt conversations have been destroyed, and while I would not claim they would provide sensational revelations on the wartime strategies of the two leaders, they would give historians a unique insight into an historic relationship. I know the shredders have to begin somewhere; it just seems a pity that the Radio Department's records have vanished.

The National Archives in Washington have no record of the Washington/New York terminal that was handled by the AT&T who too, somewhat surprisingly, have no knowledge of their end of the operation, only of the technical know-how of the A3 Scrambler system. That we were comparatively successful in our objectives only emerged many years later with the publication of David Kahn's book, *The Codebreakers*.

Despite the original excitement of the Germans when they tapped into our A3 Scramblers, at the end of the day, contrary to their expectations, they gained little original Intelligence from them, and the results from what they considered a top-level electronic breakthrough were disappointing.

So perhaps I have unfairly blamed the Colonel for his, at times, almost laughable obsession with secrecy. Perhaps he too knew little of our enemy's whereabouts and potential and was taking no chances. We seem to have been unknowing participants in a sort of private war being fought out by our own GPO, AT&T and the Deutscher Reichpost.

The British, the Americans and the Germans could all claim some success in the infant field of electronic surveillance and voice-privacy techniques. There was the German effort at breaking through the A3's parameters. The 'Sigsaly' system meticulously researched over many years gave the Americans much-needed speech protection in many theatres of military operations, while our own highly successful breakdown of the German signals and codes with Enigma contributed to our eventual victory.

On 8 May 1945, I rushed home, phoned up an old friend Ernest Maurice who was home on leave, and together we joined the thousands (it felt like millions) surging, singing and swaying down Whitehall, down Constitutional Hill to the Palace; it didn't matter that we didn't see the Royal Family or Churchill, all that mattered was that we had won and we had a future ahead.

I am almost ashamed to admit it, but my chief aim in those first few weeks of peace was to go to sleep at an ordinary bed-time of about 11pm and wake up again at 8am. I had no idea I was so tired and sleep-starved until I relaxed, and it took time to regain my normal sleep patterns.

My star was in the ascendancy – there was no doubt about it. Ronald was struggling home up Italy, from Greece some-how through Europe and was due to be demobbed as soon as he reached London. He had served nearly six years in the army and was to be one of the first 'out'. I met him in his 'demob suit' at the Albany Barracks near Regents Park, looking tanned, very thin and not all that well – not to worry, he had come home.

Then we started to talk. To my amazement, he knew all about the Radio Link to Cairo. When he served in Cairo he was on Mr Macmillan's staff, sat in the office next to his, and heard Mr Macmillan and General Alexander bellowing down the line to London, and cursing the impossibility of making themselves heard. I told him of Churchill's reaction when he failed to hear Mr Macmillan. We wondered if Churchill and Harold Macmillan would have handed the phone over to us … another lost opportunity!

With no work to do at Union House, as long as we signed on weekly, we were left to our own devices and to plan our future. Through our Personnel Department, I was asked if I would like the opportunity to work for Hansard as a parliamentary short-hand writer. I refused politely. Enough of working anti-social hours, I thought. I swore to myself that I never wanted to write another shorthand outline in my life (ambition achieved), for I felt as though I had taken down the whole War in shorthand, and in a manner of speaking, I suppose I had.

The question I am always asked is: 'Did you actually meet Mr Churchill?' and I have to answer 'No'. True, Churchill showed no desire to meet me, and somehow, I felt it would not be appropriate to request a meeting. I don't suppose it ever entered the Colonel's head to arrange such a thing. What I really wished for was a talk with my opposite number in Washington. I wanted to hear and compare notes about her experiences working for President Roosevelt, and most of all, I wanted to know if the Russians actually took advantage of their live link-up. I tried hard to persuade our Faraday operator to connect me, asked Bill to intercede on my behalf, but our efforts came to nought, and to this day, I still haven't got the answer.

Getting married and setting up home in 1945 was almost a full-time occupation. London was bomb-scarred, neglected, grey and dirty and finding a liveable undamaged flat needed determination, and an ability to reach any part of London at a moment's notice in order to be first in the queue. Even trying to buy such everyday objects like saucepans became a major expedition round the shops. I bartered Ronald's army shirts for an alarm clock; our mattress from Maples was obtained by queuing for several hours, then hurling ourselves onto the first likely one we could see when eventually some were delivered. Much merriment was caused by an elderly aunt who enquired if we had a wedding list she could consult.

My colleagues had returned thankfully to their homes, having had to endure uncomfortable and pokey bed-sits for the duration: Lilla to her farm near Ely; Joan Beard to Southampton; Matti Pritchard and Diana Straghan awaited husbands back from overseas service. All of us were trying to pick up the threads of our former lives. Bill had decided he wished to stand for Parliament and fought a North London constituency unsuccessfully for the Labour Party. He then got himself elected to the London County Council where he served for many years ending a distinguished career by becoming Chairman of the Decimal Currency Board, and in 1967, was created a Life Peer. Lord Fiske, as he was then known, died in 1975.

In the second week of July, on a warm summer day, I returned to Union House for the last time, and reported to the Colonel, still working in his small office. He rose as I entered and stood stiffly to attention. In his left hand were two small buff Civil Service envelopes containing my references. He shook my hand formally, handed me the envelopes and said, 'I wish you well in your future life Miss Magnus,' and sat down to resume his writing. I was dismissed.

And that was all, that was absolutely all. I had worked closely with him, day after day for over three years, during the most dramatic of times, and yet I knew nothing whatsoever about him – whether he was married, if he had children, or even exactly where he lived. He always addressed me as 'Miss Magnus', and I presume he knew my domestic details, yet he never asked me any personal questions. No doubt about it, for the Colonel, I was his 'other rank'. Yet there was another side. During those momentous years when I must have listened in to hundreds of calls made by men party to the highest confidential information, not once did he reprimand me or make any critical comment on my work, and I must have taken some dubious decisions, made wrong and hasty judgements, and worst of all, taken no initiative when it was vitally necessary to do so.

I realised he must have taken full and unquestioning responsibility not only for my position, but for the whole Department, that he had acted to his own high standards of discipline, for only then could he ensure the complete secrecy of the existence of the Radio Section. And who is to say he did not succeed? I walked out of the door into the sunlight.

And yet ... and yet ... As the years passed, there was something odd about my wartime experience, and I began to realise the unique position fate had bestowed on me because as hard as I tried, a blank wall of silence and ignorance met my enquiries about those all-important telephone calls between Churchill and Roosevelt. I had quite purposely not read many of the numerous biographies about the relationship because I wanted to keep my mind clear about the impressions I had received, the odd mention of a 'telephone link' by writers and journalists was so inaccurate as to be laughable.

So, I decided on another tack. I would try to retrieve my notes and edit them myself. I reckoned my shorthand notes would have been destroyed, but surely all those transcriptions of the talks would be stored somewhere in our official vaults or cellars. Though that wartime paper was bulky, my writing (then!) was quite legible. I spent years writing to various government departments – the Public Record Office, Cabinet Office – nobody had ever heard of either them or me, till finally the Ministry of Defence told me 'they were closed' and not likely to be opened, that is if they ever saw them or just wanted to get rid of me.

All those years ago, I had signed the Official Secrets Act and that meant to me that I could only refer openly to the service if papers relating to its existence were 'In the Public Domain'. Now I called in the Imperial War Museum and James Taylor, their very helpful librarian who, in turn, sent me to Phil Reed, director of the Cabinet War Rooms. He suggested I approach Sir Martin Gilbert, who is virtually a working computer system on his own and knows the whereabouts of every piece of paper referring to Churchill, and he located the papers setting up the Transatlantic Radio Link in Churchill's own private Wartime Files. So, I was clear to tell the world.

It proved equally hard to find evidence in the American records too. This, I think, is because the terminal was handled by AT&T, and they say they have no records though their operator did use her discretion on security subjects. Their lack of evidence and interest is probably due to the enormous technical breakthrough they achieved with the digital pulse voice-privacy system built into 'Sigsaly' while not realising their dependence on the TRL during late 1941–43.

The German Historical Association in London were helpful and interested in the London TRL and had wondered if anybody would show interest in their work and technical breakthrough cracking our A3 Scrambler codes. They regarded the Forschungsanstalt Unit a high Intelligence coup. Kurt Vetterlein died some years ago, a highly respected electronic engineer. At the time of my research, West and the former East Germany were merging their documentation of Wartime

Intelligence and I found nothing of particular relevance. Phil Reed tried valiantly on my behalf, but to no avail.

Neither the Dutch official Nederlands Instituut voor Oorlogsdocumentatie for War Documentation, nor the Military Museum has heard of the Valkesnwaard Forschungstanstalt Bureau, and I, in 2004, went on a visit to Amsterdam with my son to see the house in Ellbourg near Amsterdam where the Magnus family had left to come to England in 1774, and thought I would contact them again. This time it brought some amazing results. Though they still had no record of any military activities in Valkesnwaard, their director, Dr Hans de Vries, gave me the address of Hans Knap, a retired television journalist who had written a book (unpublished) about the German Monitoring Unit there. I contacted him immediately, he came round to my hotel and told me the extraordinary history and rivalry between the Dutch Post Office, the PPP, the German Reichpost and the British GPO dating back to the end of the nineteenth century covering the Boer War, First World War and, most importantly, the interbellum years to 1939.

Dutch hostility for Britain originated in the field of telecommunications at the beginning of the twentieth century when the British dominated the world in telegraphic communications, causing the Dutch government great unease because of their reliance on it to govern their colonies, the Dutch East Indies. Germany too had their colonies and territories to protect and it was at that point before 1914 that PPP, Telefunken, AEG and Siemens became jointly organised with German technology, but we lost the initiative to compete. By the 1920s, the Dutch had become the leaders in shortwave communications using German technology and, afraid of losing their influence over their colonies, transmissions did not cease until 1940.

By now, both German and Dutch telecommunication systems were completely integrated and jointly ran the big monitoring receiver facility in Noordwijk, covering all the telex traffic and taped telegraphy traffic of the Allies; their one obstacle to the complete domination of the airwaves was being unable to decode the A3 Scrambler. But then Kurt Vetterlein was called in, and their domination of the airwaves was complete. Now I could understand why such a large number of fluent English speakers worked there, the high levels of security surrounding the site and the ignorance of the local population in Valkesnwaard of the true purpose of this outwardly innocent-looking farm building, even with its radar masts protruding from its roof. I had wondered about the staffing levels too. Our TRL was strictly for necessary business and not a chat line. Churchill and Roosevelt exchanged pleasantries and then got down to work.

What a strange twist to history that when that intrepid journalist, 'The Young Winston', was trying to get his copy back to his London paper during the Boer War, the battle of the airwaves was just starting to hot up.

Since I went 'public' around the early 1990s and I was around seventy-five, my life has changed in a way I could never have imagined. I first started by giving talks to clubs and societies about my experiences during the Second World War, which escalated beyond belief. The highlight was being invited by The International Churchill Centre in Washington to speak at one of their conferences. (Mr Sequira would have been proud of my 'projection'.) I had a wonderful time amongst charming people, looked after by our friends Drs John and Susan Mather. I made a half-hour television film for the History Channel for Flashback TV, which won an award at an American film festival, and numerous 'spot' interviews for television. The most amusing was the exhausted camera TV crew, who had been trailing around

Blenheim Palace all morning arriving at my small cottage in the afternoon to film me in the middle of a heat wave. The most interesting was doing a slot with Walter Cronkite (the famous American wartime journalist who returned to London in 1942) in 2005 to remember the Second World War when he lived there as a war correspondent. He was ninety in 2005, a charming man, a courageous journalist, and still working.

By far the most exciting moments came for me at the opening of the Churchill Museum in February 2005 when I was presented to the Queen. Phil Reed, the director of the Cabinet War Rooms, had worked devotedly for years trying to mount a fitting tribute to our nation's 'Greatest Englishman', and when he finally persuaded the Treasury to remove their bundles from their basement, he saw his chance. As a result, the Churchill Museum is the very model of what a modern museum should be, with imaginative technology, film, images and a host of knobs to push and pull. It is in tune with today's children who love it, as I am sure Churchill himself would have done. I have to confess that if anybody told me nearly sixty years ago that I would be on a DVD in a glass case in a museum …

Writing this account of my life, I realise I have lived through two wars and a revolution. The Second World War, certainly, the struggle for supremacy of the airwaves as they existed then, bitter and unforgiving, and of course the revolution in digital and communication technology, from one radio link across the Atlantic to where every fourteen-year-old has a mobile phone. Surveillance cameras are everywhere. What is yet to come?

There has been a rumour going around for some time now. Phillips of Eindhovern developed the original flat-top reel recorders and some say there are recordings of the Churchill/ Roosevelt conversations. Would it not be fitting now for them to find their natural home in the Churchill Museum?

# LIFESTYLE NOTES

Along with 'bomb stories' came the nation's favourite topic of conversation – food and all allied subjects, either how to obtain it, cook it and how to beat it (preferably legally) – but be prepared to stretch a point or so … Rationing brought out the true entrepreneurial talents of the British people and it became a national preoccupation. In our household of two, the demarcation line was sharply drawn, my mother did the basic shopping, while I did the 'cooking' because Ma was too busy with her various committees and she had a very rare talent that was greatly in demand by sewing groups. She was a wonderful self-taught needlewoman and knew how to pin up a collar band on to a shirt and finally pin up a collar in various sizes. And army flannel is not at all easy to work. She had gone through life managing only to enter a kitchen to give orders, and that included me. I wasn't much better either, except I was hungry and I had three wonderful supports in the nearby shops: Charlie the butcher;

Mr Barnard the fishmonger; and Mr Austin the greengrocer. Between them, they kept us going. Cullen down the road supplied the points' goods.

I didn't fantasise over food, or bemoaned the loss of a good steak, roast lamb or chops and the inability to make proper pastry. What I missed desperately, dreamt about, longed for with all my heart, was *clothes*. I had always been interested in 'appearance' and style, making my own clothes. I adored the MGM film stars' outfits, and clothes rationing, with only a very limited number of yearly points allocated, was a real sensory deprivation.

The majority of us (including Churchill) had our own back-up team. Ronald had written from the desert that it was very cold at nights and would appreciate another knitted pullover. I wrote to my dear school friend Denise Dillon, who was a WREN stationed in Sydney, to send me some wool; she duly obliged by sending over some thick yarn. I knitted it up, including a balaclava helmet, which arrived by the time he was posted to Persia, where it was 107° in the shade. Denise sent me a hot-water bottle, all sorts of household replacements, and acted like a general store for us. She died tragically of cancer when she was only thirty years old.

Meanwhile, Ronald had been posted to GHQ in Cairo, a much nearer source of supplies. By 1942 my shoes were wearing out, so I drew an outline of my feet on two Airmail letters and posted them off. Back came a beautiful pair of hand-sewn walking shoes. Before I could order another pair, he had been posted to Casserta and off to the Front Line where he developed an acute appendix, having it removed in a military hospital before being sent to Capri and a life of luxury in Gracie Fields' villa to recuperate. He wrote about the charming Italian nurses, scrumptious Italian food and lemon-scented gardens. I wrote back, enviously remembering lemons, and about only a fortnight later, two huge crates of lemons arrived in Hampstead. Disposing of hundreds of lemons (on the turn) was quite a chore, though Charlie and Misters A&B were well disposed towards me after that gift. About a week later, another crate arrived – this time containing currants. Nobody was much interested and I seem to remember carting them down to St John's and Elizabeth Hospital. I implored him to cancel orders with his greengrocer. It all worked in reverse of course. Ronald smoked a pipe and a scheme operated whereby you filled in a GVT form in the UK and presented it to a tobacconist. They in turn promised to send tobacco to the addressee for a very reasonable amount a month. I thought Harrods would be the most reliable to deliver and so they proved to be. I didn't find out until 1945 that tobacco arrived monthly to Persia, Egypt, Italy and Greece, making many happy puffing soldiers. My very belated thanks must go to Harrods for their generosity.

When I started work at the Postal Censorship, I was reasonably well dressed. In August 1939, when I returned from Paris, I had brought two Guerlin lipsticks, Coty powder and compact and two cheap cotton dresses from Galleries Layfayette, and I still had them in 1945. My look had deteriorated considerably and I think I was an innovator in the 'layered look', coming on night duty wearing anything warm I could find. We had only a small electric one-bar heater, and I had heard that Churchill liked the young ladies around him to look neat, well dressed and tidy. Thank goodness he couldn't see the tramp-like female crouched by the telephone when he wanted to speak to his friend Mr Bernard Baruch at about 1am. Usually these talks were about family – they could easily have been two nice elderly gentlemen having a chat. Yet once, to my horror, Churchill started reading out a list of numbers with Bernie doing his best to get them down accurately. What on earth ... Then my dressmaking instincts took over – Churchill was giving him his own measurements. My theory is that, like so many fair-skinned folk, Churchill had sensitive skin and liked to wear silk undies, and his American friend was going to get them for him. It was this combination of homeliness, combined with his other heroic qualities, that made his character so much larger than life.

# NOTES

The Ministry of Defence assures me that no working notes of the Churchill/Roosevelt conversations have been stored, and I have to accept this. There are no references to the Radio Section or Department, or the Postal Telegraph Censorship, and in the Public Record Office, officials there tell me that probably the Department came under the fifty-year rule, so there was a chance that any records would have been released in 1995. Because the papers are not in 'the public domain', that is, accessible through the Public Records Office, I could technically be accused of contravening the Official Secrets Act.

But there are obvious allusions to the role of the censor and Churchill's personal acceptance of the rules (in his own handwriting) of the Radio Section when speaking over the Transatlantic Radio Link, which, in itself, is an acknowledgement of the Department's existence.

John Taylor of the American National Archives in Washington has no details or papers relating to the service; Professor Warren

Kimball, who has compiled a Complete Correspondence between Churchill and Roosevelt, is of the opinion that only a very few scrappy notes of their calls have survived. The US Army Files at Carlisle Barracks have no records, and more surprisingly, AT&T have only technical knowledge of handling the A3 Scrambler system during the War. I have been writing to all these material sources, but none of them seem to know who actually censored those Washington calls.

Murray Stern, a personal friend and military historian, has undertaken a nationwide computer search of published books on this subject and has drawn a complete blank. So I have to conclude that the Americans, like us, have no documentation of our joint wartime activity. Efforts to trace the censors and operators have also failed.

The chapters relating to wartime internal telephone censorship, the 100 per cent coverage of Irish lines and the military spot security checks are covered by a BT Archive paper.

The German material comes from David Kahn, Assistant Viewpoints Editor of *Newsday* (*American Times Mirror* newspaper), who has written at length about the *Forschungstelle* (Research Post) in his books *The Codebreakers* and *Hitler's Spies*. He has given me permission to quote his material.

I can supply relevant War Cabinet Papers confirming my material, which includes the setting up of the Russian Line, the War Cabinet's reactions to the installation of the American 'Sigsaly' system in the War Cabinet Room and Canadian Archival material from the Canadian National Archives.

I can show my references of character given when I left the Department. BT have promised to assemble equipment used by me then – earphones, old telephone and small switch panel – compared with the floor to ceiling technology of 'Sigsaly'. Only if needed, I have a photograph of RM, circa 1941.

# ACKNOWLEDGEMENTS & SOURCE MATERIAL

During the years it has taken me to research and write this account of a little-known Second World War department, I have gathered together a terrific band of supporters and well-wishers, and without their encouragement I could never have finished the book. Will they please forgive me for not mentioning them all personally in this note if I say how grateful I am for their advice and support? This also includes my various medical teams who have done valiant work to keep me on my feet. However, I must make some exceptions and mention some by name so I can thank them for the important role they played, for their patience and enthusiasm, and contributing vital information without which I could never have completed this book. So, a big 'thank you' to all.

David Benedictus for kick-starting the whole project some twenty years ago.

Sir Martin Gilbert who directed me to the essential Churchill papers enabling me to 'go public'.

Louise Golding and Jacqueline Pinto for their endless encouragement and faith in my cause.

Phil Reed, Director of the Cabinet War Rooms and Churchill Museums, for his unwavering support and advice, and his caring and helpful assistants who were always around when needed.

Allen Packwood, Director of Churchill Archive Centre, Churchill College, Cambridge, who was able on an immediate request to produce the correspondence between WSC and Dr Joseph Dulberg.

James Taylor of the Imperial War Museum who did vital research on my behalf.

Taylor Downing of Flashback Productions, who started my 'TV career' with his documentary programme on my WWII role.

The BBC for a few seconds on the *Today* programme – quite the scariest of all media attention – and Ivor Gaber's Radio 4 programme *Listening in to History,* which was quite the most enjoyable.

Hans Knap, a Dutch journalist whose notes on the Forschungstelle Langerveld Unit in Holland brought together many of the loose ends that puzzled me when we met for a talk in an Amsterdam hotel.

Sophie Bradshaw of The History Press, who has listened to my constant pleas to hurry up – 'I don't want the book to be posthumous'!

And finally, my gratitude and love to my two sons David and Martin, who always put up with my frustration and irritability when nobody answered my enquiring letters and came up with helpful suggestions, advice and all-round comfort.

## Source Material

*United Kingdom*
British Telecom; Archives and Museum
Imperial War Museum
Cabinet War Rooms and Churchill Museum
Public Records Office
Churchill Archive Centre, Churchill College, Cambridge
Winston Churchill, *On Jewish Problems* published for The
    World Jewish Congress in 1956

*Canada*
Canadian National Archives

*America*
The National Archives of US
AT&T
The Bell Telephone Co.
Robert Price of *Spectrum Magazine*
David Kahn, author of *The Codebreakers* (Macmillan, New
    York)

*Germany*
The German Historical Institute, Bloomsbury Square, London
Professor Jurgen Rohwer of Stuttgart University

*Holland*

Joop van den Linden of the Valkenswaard Heritage Society
(photographs of the Arts Centre and map of the area)

The Valkenswaard Heritage Centre

Hans Knap (unpublished papers on the Forschungstelle Langveld
Unit operating in Noordwijk and Valkenswaard, 1941–45)

Nederlands Instituut voor Oorlogsdocumentatie, Amsterdam

# APPENDIX:
# CHURCHILL DOCUMENTS

*248 4*

The records of radio telephone conversations - particularly with Washington - reported by the Censors, still contain instances of gross lack of discretion. All officers should be reminded that phrases used casually in radio telephone conversations may, if pieced together by an enemy Intelligence Service, be of much greater value to the enemy than would appear from the context.

It would also seem that more use might be made of the procedure of telegraphing in cypher a memorandum in short numbered paragraphs, and then conducting the conversation by reference to those paragraphs.

(Signed) E. E. BRIDGES

19th March, 1942.

Memo from Edward Bridges expressing his frustration at continued security lapses in international calls. (Courtesy of The National Archives, UK.)

WF

8

– SECRET –

251

**PRIME MINISTER.**

I enclose a Memorandum submitted by the Chairman of the Wireless Telegraphy Board, who are perturbed at the use made of radio telephony and ask that instructions should be issued that no information of value to the enemy is ever transmitted over the radio telephone.

The most effective way of bringing this warning home would be if you would mention the matter to a Meeting of the War Cabinet and give instructions to Ministers to bring this matter to the notice of their staffs, and to take effective steps to secure its observance.

*Circulate*

*A.*
*& put it*
*on the*
*Cab. Agenda*

*EEB*

10th March, 1942.

*P.M.*

*Please see also Mr Brockie's minute of March 10 below, which links on with this. J.M.M. 11/3*

*Duplicate noticed and returned 13.3.42.*

Memo from Edward Bridges to Churchill highlighting general concern over the security of the telegraph. (Courtesy of The National Archives, UK.)

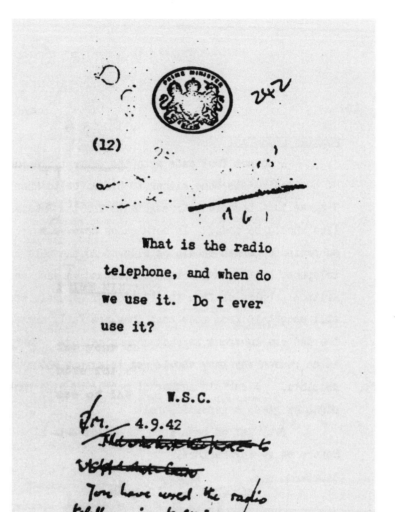

(12)

What is the radio telephone, and when do we use it. Do I ever use it?

W.S.C.

4.9.42

You have used the radio telephone in talking across the Atlantic and to Cairo.

A note from Churchill showing his desire to understand the radio telephone. (Courtesy of The National Archives, UK.)

231

# PRIME MINISTER'S
# PERSONAL MINUTE

**(5)**

Indexed

SERIAL No. M.460/2

FOREIGN SECRETARY

I do not feel safe with the present free use of the radio telephone either to U.S.A. or to Russia. I agree that technical arrangements for the Russian line should be made. In both cases however no subordinate person should be allowed to use this telephone unless they obtain beforehand in each case written permission from the Postmaster General, who will ascertain from them that they are fully aware of the dangers inherent in such communication. There is no reason why they should not telegraph whenever possible. A certain number of people of high rank might be given a general permit.

Pray let me have some scheme of this kind before we go any farther.

W.S.C.

12.10.42

Copy given to Major Morton 13.10.42.

A memo from Churchill to the Foreign Secretary expressing grave concerns over the security of calls to America and Russia. (Courtesy of The National Archives, UK.)

Abschrift.

Geheime Reichssache

SS-Hauptamt FS-Nr. 69 vom 23.7.42 10⁵⁰ .

Forschungsanstalt der Deutschen Reichspost, 23.7.42, 8⁴³ Uhr:

An

    SS-Gruppenführer Generalleutnant der Waffen-SS

        · B e r g e r,

                  B e r l i n W.35,

                  SS-Hauptamt,

mit der Bitte um absprachegemässe Weitergabe.

Laufnummer: 64,   Tag: 22.7.42,    Uhrzeit: 16.10
Rolle: 599.                  (deutsch.Sommerzeit

— — —

Gesprächsteilnehmer:

A.   New York, Mr. B u t c h e r (?),

B.   London, Whitehall 4433, Winston Churchill.

Gespräch:

Beamtin ruft wiederholt: Hallo, Mr. Churchill.

A. : Hallo, guten Morgen.

B. : Hallo, ja ich höre Sie.

Docket from Valkenswaard, showing a call between WSC and US (codenames are used). (Courtesy of David Kahn, *Newsweek*).

Also by The History Press:

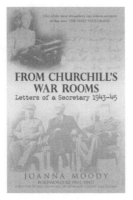

ISBN: 978-0-7524-4608-0
Paperback
£9.99

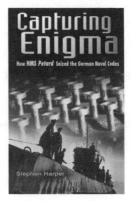

ISBN: 978-0-7509-3050-5
Paperback
£8.99

ISBN: 978-0-7509-4027-6
Hardback
£17.99

ISBN: 978-0-7509-5059-6
Hardback
£20

If you are interested in purchasing other books by The History
Press, or in case you have difficulty finding any books by The
History Press in your local bookshop, you can also place an order
directly through our website:

www.thehistorypress.co.uk